Playi

Cha

A Christmas Carol
FOR KIDS

(The melodramatic version!)

For 7-18+ actors, or kids of all ages who want to have fun!
Creatively modified by
Khara C. Barnhart and Brendan P. Kelso
Charles Dickens illustrated by Adam T. Watson
Cover characters by Ron Leishman
Special Contributor: Asif Zamir

3 Melodramatic Modifications of Dickens' Novel
for 3 different group sizes:

7-11+ Actors

12-15+ Actors

16-18+ Actors

Table Of Contents

For Zoë, Alexis, and Julian
- KCO

To Frank, our secret Santa. You always make
Christmas magical!
- BPK

Playing with Plays™ – Charles Dickens' A Christmas Carol for Kids

Copyright © 2004-2020 by Brendan P. Kelso, Playing with Plays LLC
Some characters on the cover are ©Ron Leishman ToonClipart.com

For performance rights please see page 6 of this book or contact:

contact@PlayingWithPlays.com

Foreword

When I was in high school there was something about Shakespeare that appealed to me. Not that I understood it mind you, but there were clear scenes and images that always stood out in my mind. Romeo & Juliet, "Romeo, Romeo; wherefore art thou Romeo?"; Julius Caesar, "Et tu Brute"; Macbeth, "Double, Double, toil and trouble"; Hamlet, "to be or not to be"; A Midsummer Night's Dream, all I remember about this was a wickedly cool fairy and something about a guy turning into a donkey that I thought was pretty funny. It was not until I started analyzing Shakespeare's plays as an actor that I realized one very important thing, I still didn't understand them. Seriously though, it's tough enough for adults, let alone kids. Then it hit me, why don't I make a version that kids could perform, but make it easy for them to understand with a splash of Shakespeare lingo mixed in? And voila! A melodramatic masterpiece was created! They are intended to be melodramatically fun!

THE PLAYS: There are 3 plays within this book, for three different group sizes. The reason: to allow educators or parents to get the story across to their children regardless of the size of their group. As you read through the plays, there are several lines that are highlighted. These are actual lines from the original book. I am a little more particular about the kids saying these lines verbatim. But the rest, well... have fun!

The entire purpose of this book is to instill the love of a classic story, as well as drama, into the kids.

And when you have children who have a passion for something, they will start to teach themselves, with or without school.

These plays are intended for pure fun. Please DO NOT have the kids learn these lines verbatim, that would be a complete waste of creativity. But do have them basically know their lines and improvise wherever they want as long as it pertains to telling the story. Because that is the goal of an actor: to tell the story. In A Midsummer Night's Dream, I once had a student playing Quince question me about one of her lines, "but in the actual story, didn't the Mechanicals state that 'they would hang us'?" I thought for a second and realized that she had read the story with her mom, and she was right. So I let her add the line she wanted and it added that much more fun, it made the play theirs. I have had kids throw water on the audience, run around the audience, sit in the audience, lose their pumpkin pants (size 30 around a size 15 doesn't work very well, but makes for some great humor!) and most importantly, die all over the stage. The kids love it.

One last note: if you want some educational resources, loved our plays, want to tell the world how much your kids loved performing Shakespeare, want to insult someone with our Shakespeare Insult Generator, or are just a fan of Shakespeare, then hop on our website and have fun:

PlayingWithPlays.com

With these notes, I'll see you on the stage, have fun, and break a leg!

SCHOOL, AFTERSCHOOL, and SUMMER classes

I've been teaching these plays as afterschool and summer programs for quite some time. Many people have asked what the program is, therefore, I have put together a basic formula so any teacher or parent can follow and have melodramatic success! As well, many teachers use my books in a variety of ways. You can view the formula and many more resources on my website at: PlayingWithPlays.com

- Brendan

OTHER PLAYS AND FULL LENGTH SCRIPTS

We have over 25 different titles, as well as a full-length play in 4-acts for theatre groups: Shakespeare's Hilarious Tragedies. You can see all of our other titles on our website here: PlayingWithPlays.com/books

As well, you can see a sneak peek at some of those titles at the back of this book.

And, if you ever have any questions, please don't hesitate to ask at: Contact@PlayingWithPlays.com

ROYALTIES

If you have any questions about royalties or performance licenses, here are the basic guidelines:

1) Please contact us! We always LOVE to hear about a school or group performing our books! We would also love to share photos and brag about your program as well! (with your permission, of course)

2) If you are a group and DO NOT charge your kids to be in this production, contact us about discounted copyright fees (one way or another, we will make this work for you!) You are NOT required to buy a book per kid (but, we will still send you some really cool Shakespeare tattoos for your kids!)

3) If you are a group and DO charge your kids to be in the production, (i.e. afterschool program, summer camp) we ask that you purchase a book per kid. Contact us as we will give you a bulk discount (10 books or more) and send some really cool press on Shakespeare tattoos!

4) If you are a group and DO NOT charge the audience to see the plays, please see our website FAQs to see if you are eligible to waive the performance royalties (most performances are eligible).

5) If you are a group and DO charge the audience to see the performance, please see our website FAQs for performance licensing fees (this includes performances for donations and competitions).

Any other questions or comments, please see our website or email us at:

contact@PlayingWithPlays.com

The 15-Minute or so
A Christmas Carol for Kids

By Charles Dickens

Creatively modified by

Khara C. Barnhart and Brendan P. Kelso

7-11+ Actors

CAST OF CHARACTERS:

EBENEZER SCROOGE: greedy, grumpy, odious, old man who has a lot of money

BOB CRATCHIT: happy man - works for the greedy man

MRS. CRATCHIT: Bob's happy wife

[1]**TINY TIM**: Bob's youngest happy son, who walks with a crutch

[2]**FRED**: Scrooge's nephew (he's happy too!)

[3]**YOUNG SCROOGE**: The Scrooge of the past

[1]**FEZZIWIG**: Scrooge's old boss

[4]**BELLE**: Scrooge's old girlfriend

[2]**THE GHOST OF CHRISTMAS PAST**: ghost from the past

[3]**THE GHOST OF CHRISTMAS PRESENT**: ghost from today

[4]**THE GHOST OF CHRISTMAS YET TO COME**: ghost from the future

SCHOOL CHILDREN: Classmates in Scrooge's past (all actors play CHILDREN when not playing other roles)

VILLAGERS: Attend Fezziwig's Christmas party and have small speaking roles. They provide background for various other scenes (all actors play VILLAGERS while not playing other roles)

The same actors can play the following parts:

[1]TINY TIM and FEZZIWIG

[2]FRED and GHOST OF CHRISTMAS PAST

[3]YOUNG SCROOGE and GHOST OF CHRISTMAS PRESENT

[4]BELLE and GHOST OF CHRISTMAS YET TO COME

BONUS: If there are 8 or more actors, you can add **Marley** to the small play. Use Act 1 Scene 2 from the medium play - **Marley** will also play a villager with a speaking part.

ACT 1 SCENE 1

(enter SCROOGE and BOB)

BOB: Cold! It's sooo cold!

SCROOGE: Toughen up, there, Bob! Get back to work!

BOB: Yes, Mr. Scrooge.

(enter FRED)

FRED: *(very loud and happy)* A Merry Christmas, Uncle!

SCROOGE: *(very grumpy)* Bah! Humbug! There's no reason for you to be happy! You're poor enough.

FRED: And there's no reason for you to be so cranky! You're rich enough!

SCROOGE: Bah! Humbug! Every idiot who goes around with 'Merry Christmas' on his lips should be boiled in his own pudding and buried with a stake of holly though his heart.

FRED: That's gross.

SCROOGE: *(mean)* Well, that's what it says in the book! And you know what? I believe it, too!

FRED: *(to the audience)* Well, it's still gross. *(to SCROOGE)* Look, why don't you come to my house for Christmas dinner. It'll be fun!

SCROOGE: Not going to happen.

FRED: Whatever. Have fun being miserable. *(starts acting like Scrooge behind his back; BOB laughs)* Merry Christmas, Bob!

(FRED exits)

BOB: Merry Christmas to you, Fred! *(to SCROOGE)* Mr. Scrooge? A man came in earlier and asked if you might give some of your money to the poor. You know, for food and stuff.

SCROOGE: *(to the audience)* Seriously? Give money to the poor? Who would THINK of such a thing! No way!

BOB: *(to audience)* Well, I tried...

SCROOGE: Time to go home, Bob. You'll want ALL day tomorrow, I suppose?

BOB: It IS Christmas, sir. Just saying.

SCROOGE: It IS ridiculous. And it's not fair. I have to pay you for NOT working and that makes me so mad! *(stomps up and down)*

BOB: Uh, sorry. Bye. *(to audience)* Wow, he has some real anger issues! I think he needs some counseling!

(BOB and SCROOGE exit opposite sides of stage)

ACT 1 SCENE 2*

*(if 8 or more actors, Act 1 Scene 2 from the medium play can be used)

(enter SCROOGE)

SCROOGE: *(to audience)* I must be going crazy! My old business partner, Jacob Marley, just showed up as a ghost. I don't even believe in ghosts! He died seven years ago, this very night. He started yelling about this HUGE chain he has to lug around in the afterworld because he was mean. He said my chain would be even bigger! He even used the word, ponderous! Humbug! Oh right, he also said that I'd be haunted by three spirits. Give me a break! I've never heard something so ridiculous in my entire life. Well, time for bed. *(he lies down on the floor and a bell starts ringing loudly, then there is the sound of loud footsteps offstage getting louder and louder)* It's humbug still! I won't believe it.

(SCROOGE goes to sleep)

ACT 2 SCENE 1

(enter GHOST OF CHRISTMAS PAST)

GHOST PAST: Ahem! *(waits a few seconds then starts waving his hands)* AHEM!!!!!!!

SCROOGE: Aghhhhhh!!!! *(startled and jumps up off the floor)* Who, and what are you?

GHOST PAST: I am the Ghost of Christmas Past.

SCROOGE: *(to audience)* Aw, man, that Marley ghost was real! What a downer.

GHOST PAST: Look, we've got a lot of work to do and not much time, so let's go.

(GHOST PAST drags SCROOGE around the stage in a zig-zag)

SCROOGE: *(looking around, out of balance)* Wait a minute! I'm dizzy...hey, this is where I grew up. *(pointing at himself)* Hey, that's me!

(enter SCHOOL CHILDREN and YOUNG SCROOGE, laughing and playing tag; all of the children start picking on YOUNG SCROOGE; All SCHOOL CHILDREN run offstage leaving YOUNG SCROOGE onstage ...sad; he then follows them offstage)

GHOST PAST: *(laughing)* Whoa. That's harsh.

SCROOGE: *(really bummed)* They were so mean to me!

GHOST PAST: Kind of like the way you treat people today, right?

SCROOGE: But I was just a kid!

GHOST PAST: Yeah, stinks to be you. Come on, more to see...

(enter FEZZIWIG)

SCROOGE: Why it's old Fezziwig. He was my boss when I was young, and look, he's alive again!

GHOST PAST: Right. That's kind of the whole point to this going back in time thing.

(SCROOGE shoots another glare at GHOST PAST)

FEZZIWIG: Let's dance! *(enter VILLAGERS and YOUNG SCROOGE; everyone starts clapping, laughing and dancing around FEZZIWIG who is acting like a conductor and waving his arms around)* Okay, listen up! *(everyone freezes)* It's time to go home, but I want everyone to have a super duper Merry Christmas. No excuses! *(ALL exit except YOUNG SCROOGE, SCROOGE and GHOST PAST)*

GHOST PAST: That Fezziwig was a cool guy. He made everyone feel so happy, didn't he?

SCROOGE: His power lies in words and looks. *(SCROOGE is deep in thought)*

GHOST PAST: What is the matter?

SCROOGE: *(turning away from GHOST PAST)* Nothing particular.

GHOST PAST: Something, I think? Come on.... Let it out... you can do it...

SCROOGE: No... *(mutters to himself)* Okay, maybe I should have been just a little nicer to Bob...

GHOST PAST: MAYBE?

(enter BELLE)

BELLE: *(really mad to YOUNG SCROOGE)* I'm totally breaking up with you because you used to love me, but now you just love money. *(throws money in the air, and SCROOGE starts running around grabbing it)* And you're mean! Hope you have a nice life, **WITHOUT ME!** See ya! *(she begins to exit)*

YOUNG SCROOGE: Wait, Belle, I do love money, but I love you! ...and....I love money....but, no...I love you too! *(sees more money on the ground)* But, the money.... *(starts picking up money; BELLE turns, does a final wave, and exits)*

YOUNG SCROOGE and SCROOGE: *(realizing Belle just left)* Nooooooo! *(YOUNG SCROOGE exits, and picks up more money on the way out)*

SCROOGE: Spirit! Why do you delight to torture me? No more! *(sees a dollar bill on the ground and picks it up)*

GHOST PAST: *(noticing SCROOGE)* Really? *(SCROOGE drops money)* Belle got married. You didn't. She had a family. You didn't. You missed out, man. Starting to get the picture?

SCROOGE: Yes, yes, yes!!! Now, make it stop!

GHOST PAST: Fine, fine. Let's go, you little crybaby. You should probably get some sleep.

SCROOGE: Sounds good to me.

(SCROOGE lies back on the floor and falls asleep; GHOST PAST tiptoes offstage)

ACT 2 SCENE 2

(enter GHOST PRESENT wearing a robe and holding a turkey leg and a goblet)

GHOST PRESENT: Wake up, Scrooge! I am the Ghost of Christmas Present. Look upon me!

SCROOGE: I'm looking. Not that impressed. But let's get on with it.

GHOST PRESENT: Touch my robe! *(SCROOGE touches GHOST PRESENT's robe; pause; they look at each other)* Er...it must be broken. Guess we walk. Come on. *(they begin walking downstage)*

SCROOGE: Where are we going?

GHOST PRESENT: Your employee, Bob Cratchit's house. Oh look, here we are.

(enter BOB, MRS. CRATCHIT, and TINY TIM, who has a crutch in one hand; they are all holding bowls)

BOB: *(to audience)* Hi, we're the Cratchit family. We are a REALLY happy family!

MRS. CRATCHIT: *(to audience)* Yes, but we're REALLY poor, too. Thanks to HIS boss! *(pointing at BOB)* As you can see, our bowls are empty. *(they all show empty bowls)* We practically survive off air.

TINY TIM: *(to audience)* But we're happy!

MRS. CRATCHIT: *(to audience; overly sappy)* Because we have each other.

TINY TIM: And love!

SCROOGE: *(to GHOST PRESENT)* Seriously, are they for real?

GHOST PRESENT: Yep! Adorable, isn't it?

BOB: A merry Christmas to us all.

TINY TIM: God bless us every one!

SCROOGE: Spirit, tell me if Tiny Tim will live.

GHOST PRESENT: *(puts hands to head as if looking into the future)* Ooooo, not so good....I see a vacant seat in the poor chimney corner, and a crutch without an owner. If SOMEBODY doesn't change SOMETHING, the child will die.

SCROOGE: No, no! Say he will be spared.

GHOST PRESENT: Nope, can't do that, sorry. Unless SOMEONE decides to change...hint, hint.

BOB: A Christmas toast to my boss, Mr. Scrooge! The founder of the feast!

MRS. CRATCHIT: *(angrily)* Oh sure, Mr. Scrooge! If he were here I'd give him a piece of my mind to feast upon. What an odious, stingy, hard, unfeeling man!

BOB: Dear, it's Christmas day. He's not THAT bad. *(Pause)* He's just... THAT sad. *(BOB holds up his bowl)* Come on, a toast to Scrooge!

TINY TIM: *(holding up his bowl)* To Scrooge!

MRS. CRATCHIT: *(muttering)* Thanks for nothing.

BOB: *(to MRS. CRATCHIT)* That's not nice.

TINY TIM: And we Cratchits are ALWAYS nice. Read the book, Mom.

MRS. CRATCHIT: Sorry, guys.

(the CRATCHIT FAMILY exits)

SCROOGE: She called me odious! Do I really smell that bad?

GHOST PRESENT: Odious doesn't mean you stink. Although in this case you do... According to the dictionary, odious means "unequivocally detestable." I mean, you are a toad sometimes Mr. Scrooge.

SCROOGE: Wow... that's kind of ... mean.

GHOST PRESENT: You are starting to get it; that's why the word "Scrooge" is associated with horrible people. Come on, we're not done. *(GHOST PRESENT and SCROOGE slowly walk across the stage; as they do, VILLAGERS appear onstage and sing a Christmas carol softly in the background)*

SCROOGE: *(moving around the people like they have some horrible virus or something)* These people are poor! And sick! Why are they singing? I don't understand where their happiness comes from. I don't understand anything anymore. I'm sooooo confused!!!

GHOST PRESENT: That's correct, you are confused. *(to audience)* This guy is truly a piece of work. *(to SCROOGE)* Okay, we're here.

(enter FRED; the VILLAGERS stop singing and gather around FRED)

FRED: *(laughs loudly while entering)* Ha, ha, ha! He said that Christmas was a Humbug. He believed it too! *(everyone laughs)* He's not very nice. I mean, some might even call him... odious!

SCROOGE: *(to GHOST PRESENT)* He's talking about me, isn't he?

GHOST PRESENT: What gave it away, the humbug or the odious comment? *(SCROOGE makes a face at GHOST PRESENT)*

VILLAGER: But he's SUPER rich! Seriously, I mean a LOT of money!

FRED: So what? He don't do any good with it. He don't make himself comfortable with it. But I am sorry for him. He's only making himself miserable, not us! Ha! Poor old Scrooge. But, he is fun to laugh at!

VILLAGER #2: I know, let's play a game. How 'bout YES and NO? You go first, Fred.

FRED: Okay! *(the VILLAGERS gather to one side of FRED)*

VILLAGER: Are you an animal?

FRED: Yes!

VILLAGER #2: Are you a bear?

FRED: No.

VILLAGER: A cat?

FRED: No.

VILLAGER #2: A cow, no wait, a pig?

FRED: No! *(starts stomping around the stage making frightening animal noises; everyone starts laughing)*

VILLAGER: I know what it is, Fred! It's your uncle Scro-o-o-o-oge!

FRED: Yes! *(everyone laughs more, even SCROOGE laughs a little)* He deserves a toast. To Uncle Scrooge!

VILLAGERS: *(everyone raises their hands to toast)* Uncle Scrooge! *(FRED and VILLAGERS exit)*

SCROOGE: *(to GHOST PRESENT)* I don't know whether to laugh or cry.

GHOST PRESENT: It will take a lot of laughter AND a lot of tears to unfreeze that cold heart of yours. I'd get to it if I were you since this play's almost over, and I'm done here. Later 'gator.

(GHOST PRESENT taps SCROOGE on the head and SCROOGE falls immediately asleep; GHOST PRESENT exits)

ACT 3 SCENE 1

(Enter GHOST OF CHRISTMAS YET TO COME dressed in a black gown acting all ghostly-like; shakes SCROOGE vigorously)

SCROOGE: *(wakes up startled)* Who goes there! *(sees GHOST who waves at SCROOGE)* Let me guess. You're the Ghost of Christmas Yet to Come?

(GHOST YET TO COME gives him two thumbs up)

SCROOGE: Not a big talker, are ya?

(GHOST YET TO COME shakes his head "no" and points to two VILLAGERS who have entered upstage; GHOST YET TO COME shoves SCROOGE towards the VILLAGERS)

VILLAGER #1: I don't know much about it. I only know he's dead.

VILLAGER #2: What did he do with his money?

VILLAGER #1: Who knows. He didn't leave it to me. *(VILLAGERS laugh)*

VILLAGER #2: Well you know no one will be at HIS funeral. And I heard that some poor people went through his house and took a bunch of his stuff after he died. He didn't have any family or friends there to stop them. He died sad and alone.

VILLAGER #1: Nobody liked him anyway. I hear he was odious! Good riddance, I say! *(VILLAGERS exit)*

SCROOGE: Hmmmm. That's awful. I'd hate to be THAT person, because I know what odious means now...I wonder who they're talking about.

(GHOST YET TO COME shakes head dramatically and points to the other side of the stage where BOB and MRS. CRATCHIT enter)

MRS. CRATCHIT: *(to audience)* Our Tiny Tim is gone. Dead!

BOB: *(melodramatically crying)* My little, little child!

MRS. CRATCHIT: *(crying)* His new home is in the ground. If only we had just a LITTLE money, we could have saved him! *(she looks over at SCROOGE)*

SCROOGE: *(taken aback; to GHOST YET TO COME)* Hey, can she see me? *(GHOST YET TO COME shakes his head, "no")* This is so depressing; this is supposed to be a comedy! *(to GHOST YET TO COME)* Can't we skip this part?

(GHOST YET TO COME shakes head "no")

SCROOGE: Yeah, I didn't think so.

BOB: None of us must ever forget our dear Tiny Tim!

MRS. CRATCHIT: Never!

BOB: That makes me happy.

(CRATCHITS exit)

SCROOGE: This is an awful future. I don't like it at all! Can't we stop this?

GHOST YET TO COME: NO!

SCROOGE: *(shocked)* HEY! Wait a minute, I thought you couldn't talk!

GHOST YET TO COME: Yeah, well, you just weren't getting the point, were you?!?! *(to audience)* I'm usually so spooky!!!

SCROOGE: Okay, what's next? Lay it on me; I can take it!

(GHOST YET TO COME nods and claps hands; when nothing happens he claps his hands again; a VILLAGER runs onstage, places a cardboard headstone down and runs offstage)

SCROOGE: What's that? *(he runs to headstone and picks it up; it says "EBENEZER SCROOGE" in big letters)* Nooooooooo!!! Am I the sad, pathetic, odious, DEAD man they were talking about earlier?

EVERYONE BACKSTAGE: YES!!!

(GHOST YET TO COME nods head and gives him two thumbs up)

SCROOGE: Oh no, no! I can change! I will honor Christmas in my heart, and try to keep it all the year. I will live in the Past, the Present, and the Future. I will not shut out the lessons they teach. Please! Pretty, pretty please! Give me a chance. *(SCROOGE starts crying melodramatically and throws himself on the floor like he's five and having a tantrum)*

(GHOST YET TO COME pats SCROOGE on the back and then raises arms up in the air like a champion who just won a game; he gives SCROOGE a big thumbs up, waves "bye" at audience and then exits)

SCROOGE: *(stops crying and looks around)* Why, I'm home! It's my bed and my room! I am as light as a feather, I am as happy as an angel, I am as merry as a schoolboy. A merry Christmas to everybody! *(points to some random audience member)* Even you, random audience member! A happy New Year to all the world. *(he starts laughing like a crazy person and skips around the stage; a VILLAGER enters)*

SCROOGE: Hey you! What's today?

VILLAGER: Um, seriously? Why, it's Christmas Day.

SCROOGE: Woooo-hooooo!

VILLAGER: *(VILLAGER thinks he's crazy)* Yeah...woo-hoo. *(VILLAGER starts to exit)*

SCROOGE: Wait! If I give you some money, will you do me a favor? Go buy the biggest turkey you can find and take it to the Cratchit family. *(SCROOGE gives VILLAGER some money)*

VILLAGER: Really? Consider it done. Thanks!

(VILLAGER exits; FRED enters)

SCROOGE: Fred! I have come to dinner for Christmas! It'll be fun!

FRED: Fun?!?! Wow! How unbelievably awesome! If you weren't standing in front of me, I wouldn't believe you're my uncle! *(they laugh)*

SCROOGE: I know, right? And guess what? Later I'm going to give away a bunch of my money to the poor! This is the best day ever. Okay, let's go eat!

(they exit)

(enter BOB and SCROOGE from opposite sides of the stage)

SCROOGE: *(VERY serious)* You're late, Bob!

BOB: *(his head bowed down doesn't see SCROOGE smile and laugh at audience)* I am very sorry, sir.

SCROOGE: You better be! *(giggles to the audience like a kid)* I am not going to stand this sort of thing any longer. And therefore...*(SCROOGE raises his arm as though he's going to hit BOB)* I am about to raise your salary!

BOB: Say what?!?!

SCROOGE: HA! Didn't see that coming, did you? *(SCROOGE starts doing some type of money dance, while giggling to himself)*

BOB: *(shocked)* Who are you, and what have you done with Mr. Scrooge?

SCROOGE: A merry Christmas, Bob! I'm going to give you more money, I'm going to help your family, and I'm going to be a good person from now on. Isn't that great?

BOB: I can't believe it! This is totally weird, but so cool!

SCROOGE: Right?

(TINY TIM enters)

TINY TIM: God bless us, every one!

(ALL exit)

THE END

The 20-Minute or so
A Christmas Carol for Kids

By Charles Dickens

Creatively modified by

Khara C. Barnhart and Brendan P. Kelso

12-15+ Actors

CAST OF CHARACTERS:

EBENEZER SCROOGE: greedy, grumpy, odious, old man who has a lot of money

BOB CRATCHIT: happy man - works for the greedy man

MRS. CRATCHIT: Bob's happy wife

MARTHA CRATCHIT: Bob's oldest happy daughter

[1]**TINY TIM:** Bob's youngest happy son, who walks with a crutch

FRED: Scrooge's nephew (he's happy too!)

FRED'S WIFE: Fred's wife

YOUNG SCROOGE: The Scrooge of the past

JACOB MARLEY'S GHOST: used to be Scrooge's business partner

[1]**FEZZIWIG:** Scrooge's old boss

[2]**BELLE:** Scrooge's old girlfriend

THE GHOST OF CHRISTMAS PAST: ghost from the past

[3]**THE GHOST OF CHRISTMAS PRESENT:** ghost from today

[2]**THE GHOST OF CHRISTMAS YET TO COME:** ghost from the future

[3]**PORTLY MAN:** He raises money for the poor

SCHOOL CHILDREN: Classmates in Scrooge's past (all actors play CHILDREN when not playing other roles)

VILLAGERS: Attend Fezziwig's Christmas party and provide background for various other scenes (all actors play VILLAGERS while not playing other roles; some lines)

The same actors can play the following parts:

[1]TINY TIM and FEZZIWIG

[2]BELLE and GHOST OF CHRISTMAS YET TO COME

[3]GHOST OF CHRISTMAS PRESENT and PORTLY MAN

ACT 1 SCENE 1

(enter SCROOGE and BOB)

BOB: Cold! It's sooo cold!

SCROOGE: Toughen up, there, Bob! Get back to work!

BOB: Yes, Mr. Scrooge.

(enter FRED)

FRED: *(very loud and happy)* A Merry Christmas, Uncle!

SCROOGE: *(very grumpy)* Bah! Humbug! There's no reason for you to be happy! You're poor enough.

FRED: And there's no reason for you to be so cranky! You're rich enough!

SCROOGE: Bah! Humbug! Every idiot who goes around with 'Merry Christmas' on his lips should be boiled in his own pudding and buried with a stake of holly though his heart.

FRED: That's gross.

SCROOGE: *(mean)* Well, that's what it says in the book! And you know what? I believe it, too!

FRED: *(to the audience)* Well, it's still gross. *(to SCROOGE)* Look, why don't you come to my house for Christmas dinner. It'll be fun!

SCROOGE: Not going to happen.

FRED: Whatever. Have fun being miserable. *(starts acting like Scrooge behind his back; BOB laughs)* Merry Christmas, Bob!

BOB: Merry Christmas to you, Fred!

(FRED exits; enter PORTLY MAN)

PORTLY MAN: Scrooge and Marley's, I believe. Have I the pleasure of addressing Mr. Scrooge, or Mr. Marley?

SCROOGE: Mr. Marley is dead. He died seven years ago, this very night.

PORTLY MAN: Bummer. I'll keep this short. You have a lot of money, and we want you to give some to the poor. You know, for food and stuff.

SCROOGE: *(to the audience)* Seriously? Give money to the poor? Who would THINK of such a thing! *(very demanding)* No way! Leave me alone and get out of my building!

(SCROOGE shoves PORTLY MAN offstage)

SCROOGE: Time to go home, Bob. You'll want ALL day tomorrow, I suppose?

BOB: It IS Christmas, sir. Just saying.

SCROOGE: It IS ridiculous. And it's not fair. I have to pay you for NOT working and that makes me so mad! *(stomps up and down)*

BOB: Uh, sorry. Bye. *(to audience)* Wow, he has some real anger issues! I think he needs some counseling!

(BOB and SCROOGE exit opposite sides of stage)

(enter SCROOGE with MARLEY'S GHOST wondering spookily around in the background, unseen by SCROOGE)

SCROOGE: *(muttering to himself)* I must be going crazy; I thought I saw old dead Marley's face on my door. Humbug! Oh well. Time for bed. *(he lies down on the floor and a bell starts ringing loudly, then there is the sound of loud footsteps offstage getting louder and louder)* It's humbug still! I won't believe it.

(enter MARLEY'S GHOST with a chain around his waist making moaning ghost like sounds)

MARLEY: What's up, Scroooooooooooge?!

SCROOGE: *(shocked)* Jacob Marley?!?! What do you want with me?

MARLEY: Ahhhhhhhhh!!! OOOOOOOOOO!!!!!! *(shakes chains)*

SCROOGE: *(screaming)* You're so scary! And you're dead! This is NOT happening!

MARLEY: *(to audience)* This is fun! *(to SCROOGE)* Yes, it IIIIIIIISSS happening. See this chain? SEEEEEEEEE IT??! Yeah, that's all the bad stuff I did when IIIIIIIIIIII was alive. You should see youuuuuuuuur chain! It's a ponderous chain!

SCROOGE: Ponderous?

MARLEY: Yes, VERY, VEEEEEEERY BIG!!!!

SCROOGE: Oh, that's not good. Old Jacob Marley, tell me more. Speak comfort to me, Jacob!

MARLEY: I have none to give. But listen up, pal. You don't have to turn out like me! Tonight you will be haunted by Three Spirits. You have to listen to them, okay? *(pauses waiting for an answer)* OKAY?! *(starts moaning and shaking chains)*

SCROOGE: *(really scared)* I'd rather not. *(MARLEY shakes chains dramatically at SCROOGE)* OKAY!

(MARLEY exits)

SCROOGE: Man, he was pushy! And I'm sure it's just my imagination acting up; ghosts aren't real. I'm going to bed!

(SCROOGE goes to sleep on stage)

ACT 2 SCENE 1

(enter GHOST OF CHRISTMAS PAST)

GHOST PAST: Ahem! *(waits a few seconds then starts waving his hands)* AHEM!!!!!!!

SCROOGE: Aghhhhhh!!!! *(startled and jumps up off the floor)* Who, and what are you?

GHOST PAST: I am the Ghost of Christmas Past.

SCROOGE: *(to audience)* Aw, man, that Marley ghost was real! What a downer.

GHOST PAST: Look, we've got a lot of work to do and not much time, so let's go.

(GHOST PAST drags SCROOGE around the stage in a zig-zag)

SCROOGE: *(looking around, out of balance)* Wait a minute! I'm dizzy...hey, this is where I grew up. *(pointing at himself)* Hey, that's me!

(enter SCHOOL CHILDREN and YOUNG SCROOGE, laughing and playing tag; all of the children start picking on YOUNG SCROOGE; All SCHOOL CHILDREN run offstage leaving YOUNG SCROOGE onstage ...sad; he then follows them offstage)

GHOST PAST: *(laughing)* Whoa. That's harsh.

SCROOGE: *(really bummed)* They were so mean to me!

GHOST PAST: Kind of like the way you treat people today, right?

SCROOGE: But I was just a kid!

GHOST PAST: Yeah, stinks to be you. Come on, more to see... *(enter FEZZIWIG)*

SCROOGE: Why it's old Fezziwig. He was my boss when I was young, and look, he's alive again!

GHOST PAST: Right. That's kind of the whole point to this going back in time thing.

(SCROOGE shoots another glare at GHOST PAST)

FEZZIWIG: Let's dance! *(enter VILLAGERS and YOUNG SCROOGE; everyone starts clapping, laughing and dancing around FEZZIWIG who is acting like a conductor and waving his arms around)* Okay, listen up! *(everyone freezes)* It's time to go home, but I want everyone to have a super duper Merry Christmas. No excuses! *(all exit except YOUNG SCROOGE, SCROOGE and GHOST PAST)*

GHOST PAST: That Fezziwig was a cool guy. He made everyone feel so happy, didn't he?

SCROOGE: His power lies in words and looks. *(SCROOGE is deep in thought)*

GHOST PAST: What is the matter?

SCROOGE: *(turning away from GHOST PAST)* Nothing particular.

GHOST PAST: Something, I think? Come on.... let it out...you can do it...

SCROOGE: No... *(mutters to himself)* Okay, maybe I should have been just a little nicer to Bob...

GHOST PAST: MAYBE?

(enter BELLE)

BELLE: *(really mad to YOUNG SCROOGE)* I'm totally breaking up with you because you used to love me, but now you just love money. *(throws money in the air, and SCROOGE starts running around grabbing it)* And you're mean! Hope you have a nice life, **WITHOUT ME!** See ya! *(she begins to exit)*

YOUNG SCROOGE: Wait, Belle, I do love money, but I love you! ...and....I love money....but, no...I love you too! *(sees more money on the ground)* But, the money.... *(starts picking up money; BELLE turns, does a final wave, and exits)*

YOUNG SCROOGE and SCROOGE: *(realizing Belle just left)* Nooooooo! *(YOUNG SCROOGE exits, and picks up more money on the way out)*

SCROOGE: Spirit! Why do you delight to torture me? No more! *(sees a dollar bill on the ground and picks it up)*

GHOST PAST: *(noticing SCROOGE)* Really? *(SCROOGE drops money)* Belle got married. You didn't. She had a family. You didn't. You missed out, man. Starting to get the picture?

SCROOGE: Yes, yes, yes!!! Now, make it stop!

GHOST PAST: Fine, fine. Let's go, you little crybaby. You should probably get some sleep.

SCROOGE: Sounds good to me.

(SCROOGE lies back on the floor and falls asleep; GHOST PAST tiptoes offstage)

ACT 2 SCENE 2

(enter GHOST PRESENT wearing a robe and holding a turkey leg and a goblet)

GHOST PRESENT: Wake up, Scrooge! I am the Ghost of Christmas Present. Look upon me!

SCROOGE: I'm looking. Not that impressed. But let's get on with it.

GHOST PRESENT: Touch my robe! *(SCROOGE touches GHOST PRESENT's robe; pause; they look at each other)* Er...it must be broken. Guess we walk. Come on. *(they begin walking downstage)*

SCROOGE: Where are we going?

GHOST PRESENT: Your employee, Bob Cratchit's house. Oh look, here we are.

(enter BOB, MRS. CRATCHIT, MARTHA CRATCHIT, and TINY TIM, who has a crutch in one hand; they are all holding bowls)

BOB: *(to audience)* Hi, we're the Cratchit family. We are a REALLY happy family!

MRS. CRATCHIT: *(to audience)* Yes, but we're REALLY poor, too. Thanks to HIS boss! *(pointing at BOB)*

MARTHA: *(to audience)* Yeah, as you can see our bowls are empty. *(shows empty bowl)* We practically survive off air.

TINY TIM: *(to audience)* But we're happy!

MRS. CRATCHIT: *(to audience; overly sappy)* Because we have each other.

TINY TIM: And love!

SCROOGE: *(to GHOST PRESENT)* Seriously, are they for real?

GHOST PRESENT: Yep! Adorable, isn't it?

BOB: A merry Christmas to us all.

TINY TIM: God bless us every one!

SCROOGE: Spirit, tell me if Tiny Tim will live.

GHOST PRESENT: *(puts hands to head as if looking into the future)* Ooooo, not so good....I see a vacant seat in the poor chimney corner, and a crutch without an owner. If SOMEBODY doesn't change SOMETHING, the child will die.

SCROOGE: No, no! Say he will be spared.

GHOST PRESENT: Nope, can't do that, sorry. Unless SOMEONE decides to change...hint, hint.

BOB: A Christmas toast to my boss, Mr. Scrooge! The founder of the feast!

MRS. CRATCHIT: *(angrily)* Oh sure, Mr. Scrooge! If he were here I'd give him a piece of my mind to feast upon. What an odious, stingy, hard, unfeeling man!

BOB: Dear, it's Christmas day. He's not THAT bad. *(Pause)* He's just... THAT sad. *(BOB holds up his bowl)* Come on, kids, to Scrooge! He probably needs it more than us!

MARTHA & TINY TIM: *(holding up their bowls)* To Scrooge!

MRS. CRATCHIT: *(muttering)* Thanks for nothing.

BOB: That's not nice.

MARTHA: And we Cratchits are ALWAYS nice. Read the book, Mom.

MRS. CRATCHIT: Sorry.

(the CRATCHIT FAMILY exits)

SCROOGE: She called me odious! Do I really smell that bad?

GHOST PRESENT: Odious doesn't mean you stink. Although in this case you do... According to the dictionary, odious means "unequivocally detestable." I mean, you are a toad sometimes Mr. Scrooge.

SCROOGE: Wow... that's kind of ... mean.

GHOST PRESENT: Wow, you are starting to get it, that's why the word "Scrooge" is associated with horrible people. Come on, we're not done. *(GHOST PRESENT and SCROOGE slowly walk across the stage; as they do, VILLAGERS appear onstage and sing a Christmas carol softly in the background)*

SCROOGE: *(moving around the people like they have some horrible virus or something)* These people are poor! And sick! Why are they singing? I don't understand where their happiness comes from. I don't understand anything anymore. I'm sooooo confused!!!

GHOST PRESENT: That's correct, you are confused. *(to audience)* This guy is truly a piece of work. *(to SCROOGE)* Okay, we're here.

(enter FRED and FRED'S WIFE; the VILLAGERS stop singing and gather around FRED)

FRED: *(laughs loudly while entering)* Ha, ha, ha! He said that Christmas was a Humbug. He believed it too! *(everyone laughs)*

FRED'S WIFE: More shame for him, Fred.

FRED: Well, he's not very nice. I mean, some might even call him... odious!

SCROOGE: *(to GHOST PRESENT)* They're talking about me, aren't they?

GHOST PRESENT: What gave it away, the humbug or the odious comment? *(SCROOGE makes a face at GHOST PRESENT)*

FRED'S WIFE: But he's SUPER rich! Seriously, I mean a LOT of money!

FRED: So what? He don't do any good with it. He don't make himself comfortable with it. But I am sorry for him. He's only making himself miserable, not us! Ha! Poor old Scrooge. But, he is fun to laugh at!

FRED'S WIFE: I know, let's play a game. How 'bout YES and NO? You go first, Fred.

FRED: Okay! *(the VILLAGERS and FRED'S WIFE gather to one side of FRED)*

VILLAGER #1: Are you an animal?

FRED: Yes!

VILLAGER #2: Are you a bear?

FRED: No.

VILLAGER #3: A cat?

FRED: No.

VILLAGER #4: A cow, no wait, a pig?

FRED: No! *(starts stomping around the stage making frightening animal noises; everyone starts laughing)*

FRED'S WIFE: I know what it is, Fred! It's your uncle Scro-o-o-o-oge!

FRED: Yes! *(everyone laughs more, even SCROOGE laughs a little)* He deserves a toast. To Uncle Scrooge!

VILLAGERS/FRED'S WIFE: *(everyone raises their hands to toast)* Uncle Scrooge! *(FRED, FRED'S WIFE and VILLAGERS exit)*

SCROOGE: *(to GHOST PRESENT)* I don't know whether to laugh or cry.

GHOST PRESENT: It will take a lot of laughter AND a lot of tears to unfreeze that cold heart of yours. I'd get to it if I were you, this play's almost over, and I'm done here. Later 'gator.

(GHOST PRESENT taps SCROOGE on the head and SCROOGE falls immediately asleep; GHOST PRESENT exits)

ACT 3 SCENE 1

(Enter GHOST OF CHRISTMAS YET TO COME dressed in a black gown acting all ghostly-like; shakes SCROOGE vigorously)

SCROOGE: *(wakes up startled)* Who goes there! *(sees GHOST who waves at SCROOGE)* Let me guess. You're the Ghost of Christmas Yet to Come?

(GHOST YET TO COME gives him two thumbs up)

SCROOGE: Not a big talker, are ya?

(GHOST YET TO COME shakes his head "no" and points to two VILLAGERS who have entered upstage; GHOST YET TO COME shoves SCROOGE towards the VILLAGERS)

VILLAGER #1: I don't know much about it. I only know he's dead.

VILLAGER #2: What did he do with his money?

VILLAGER #1: Who knows. He didn't leave it to me. *(VILLAGERS laugh)*

VILLAGER #2: Well you know no one will be at HIS funeral. And I heard that some poor people went through his house and took a bunch of his stuff after he died. He didn't have any family or friends there to stop them. He died sad and alone.

VILLAGER #1: Nobody liked him anyway. I hear he was odious! Good riddance, I say! *(VILLAGERS exit)*

SCROOGE: Hmmmm. That's awful. I'd hate to be THAT person, because I know what odious means now...I wonder who they're talking about.

(GHOST YET TO COME shakes head dramatically and points to the other side of the stage where BOB, MRS. CRATCHIT and MARTHA CRATCHIT enter)

MARTHA: *(to audience)* Our Tiny Tim is gone. Dead.

BOB: *(melodramatically crying)* My little, little child!

MRS. CRATCHIT: *(crying)* His new home is in the ground. If only we had just a LITTLE money, we could have saved him! *(she looks over at SCROOGE)*

SCROOGE: *(taken aback; to GHOST YET TO COME)* Hey, can she see me? *(GHOST YET TO COME shakes his head, "no")* This is so depressing; this is supposed to be a comedy! *(to GHOST YET TO COME)* Can't we skip this part?

(GHOST YET TO COME shakes head "no")

SCROOGE: Yeah, I didn't think so.

BOB: None of us must ever forget our dear Tiny Tim!

MARTHA: Never, father!

BOB: That makes me happy.

(CRATCHITS exit)

SCROOGE: This is an awful future. I don't like it at all! Can't we stop this?

GHOST YET TO COME: NO!

SCROOGE: *(shocked)* HEY! Wait a minute, I thought you couldn't talk!

GHOST YET TO COME: Yeah, well, you just weren't getting the point, were you?!?! *(to audience)* I'm usually so spooky!!!

SCROOGE: Okay, what's next? Lay it on me; I can take it!

(GHOST YET TO COME nods and claps hands; when nothing happens he claps his hands again; a VILLAGER runs onstage, places a cardboard headstone down and runs offstage)

SCROOGE: What's that? *(he runs to headstone and picks it up; it says "EBENEZER SCROOGE" in big letters)* Noooooooooo!!! Am I the sad, pathetic, odious, DEAD man they were talking about earlier?

EVERYONE BACKSTAGE: YES!!!

(GHOST YET TO COME nods head and gives him two thumbs up)

SCROOGE: Oh no, no! I can change! I will honor Christmas in my heart, and try to keep it all the year. I will live in the Past, the Present, and the Future. I will not shut out the lessons they teach. Please! Pretty, pretty please! Give me a chance. *(SCROOGE starts crying melodramatically and throws himself on the floor like he's five and having a tantrum)*

(GHOST YET TO COME pats SCROOGE on the back and then raises arms up in the air like a champion who just won a game; he gives SCROOGE a big thumbs up, waves "bye" at audience and then exits)

SCROOGE: *(stops crying and looks around)* Why, I'm home! It's my bed and my room! I am as light as a feather, I am as happy as an angel, I am as merry as a schoolboy. A merry Christmas to everybody! *(points to some random audience member)* Even you, random audience member! A happy New Year to all the world. *(he starts laughing like a crazy person and skips around the stage; a VILLAGER enters)*

SCROOGE: Hey you! What's today?

VILLAGER: Um, seriously? Why, it's Christmas Day.

SCROOGE: Woooo-hooooo!

VILLAGER: *(VILLAGER thinks he's crazy)* Yeah...woo-hoo. *(VILLAGER starts to exit)*

SCROOGE: Wait! If I give you some money, will you do me a favor? Go buy the biggest turkey you can find and take it to the Cratchit family. *(SCROOGE gives VILLAGER some money)*

VILLAGER: Really? Consider it done. Thanks! *(VILLAGER exits; enter PORTLY MAN)*

SCROOGE: Oh! It's you! Do you still need money for poor people? 'Cause I want to give you a whole bunch!

PORTLY MAN: My dear Mr. Scrooge, are you serious or just humbugging me?

SCROOGE: As serious as chocolate cake!

PORTLY MAN: Wow, chocolate cake IS serious stuff. *(a large bag of cash is thrown onstage; SCROOGE picks it up and tosses it to PORTLY MAN)*

SCROOGE: Here!

PORTLY MAN: Sweet! Thanks Scrooge!

(PORTLY MAN exits; FRED and FRED'S WIFE enter)

SCROOGE: Fred! And Fred's wife! What is your name, anyway? Dickens really dropped the ball there. Anyway, I have come to dinner! It'll be fun!

FRED: Fun?!?! Wow! How unbelievably awesome! If you weren't standing in front of me, I wouldn't believe you're my uncle! *(they laugh)*

FRED'S WIFE: Let's go eat!

(ALL exit)

ACT 3 SCENE 3

(enter BOB and SCROOGE from opposite sides of the stage)

SCROOGE: *(VERY serious)* You're late, Bob!

BOB: *(his head bowed down doesn't see SCROOGE smile and laugh at audience)* I am very sorry, sir.

SCROOGE: You better be! *(giggles to the audience like a kid)* I am not going to stand this sort of thing any longer. And therefore...*(SCROOGE raises his arm as though he's going to hit BOB)* I am about to raise your salary!

BOB: Say what?!?!

SCROOGE: HA! Didn't see that coming, did you? *(SCROOGE starts doing some type of money dance, while giggling to himself)*

BOB: *(shocked)* Who are you, and what have you done with Mr. Scrooge?

SCROOGE: A merry Christmas, Bob! I'm going to give you more money, I'm going to help your family, and I'm going to be a good person from now on. Isn't that great?

BOB: I can't believe it! This is totally weird, but so cool!

SCROOGE: Right?

(TINY TIM enters)

TINY TIM: God bless us, every one!

(ALL exit)

THE END

The 25-Minute or so
A Christmas Carol for Kids

By Charles Dickens

Creatively modified by

Khara C. Barnhart and Brendan P. Kelso

16-18+ Actors

CAST OF CHARACTERS:

EBENEZER SCROOGE: greedy, grumpy, odious, old man who has a lot of money

BOB CRATCHIT: happy man - works for the greedy man

MRS. CRATCHIT: Bob's happy wife

PETER CRATCHIT: Bob's oldest happy son

MARTHA CRATCHIT: Bob's oldest happy daughter

[1]**TINY TIM:** Bob's youngest happy son, who walks with a crutch

FRED: Scrooge's nephew (he's happy too!)

FRED'S WIFE: Fred's wife

FAN: Scrooge's sister and Fred's mother

YOUNG SCROOGE: The Scrooge of the past

JACOB MARLEY'S GHOST: used to be Scrooge's business partner

[1]**FEZZIWIG:** Scrooge's old boss

BELLE: Scrooge's old girlfriend

THE GHOST OF CHRISTMAS PAST: ghost from the past

[2]**THE GHOST OF CHRISTMAS PRESENT:** ghost from today

THE GHOST OF CHRISTMAS YET TO COME: ghost from the future

[2]**PORTLY MAN #1:** He raises money for the poor

PORTLY MAN #2: He raises more money for the poor

SCHOOL CHILDREN: Classmates in Scrooge's past

VILLAGERS: Attend Fezziwig's Christmas party and provide background for various other scenes; some lines

The same actors can play the following parts:

[1]TINY TIM and FEZZIWIG

[2]GHOST OF CHRISTMAS PRESENT and PORTLY MAN #1

ACT 1 SCENE 1

(enter SCROOGE and BOB)

BOB: Cold! It's sooo cold!

SCROOGE: Toughen up, there, Bob! Get back to work!

BOB: Yes, Mr. Scrooge.

(enter FRED)

FRED: *(very loud and happy)* A Merry Christmas, Uncle!

SCROOGE: *(very grumpy)* Bah! Humbug! There's no reason for you to be happy! You're poor enough.

FRED: And there's no reason for you to be so cranky! You're rich enough!

SCROOGE: Bah! Humbug! Every idiot who goes around with 'Merry Christmas' on his lips should be boiled in his own pudding and buried with a stake of holly though his heart.

FRED: That's gross.

SCROOGE: *(mean)* Well, that's what it says in the book! And you know what? I believe it, too!

FRED: *(to the audience)* Well, it's still gross. *(to SCROOGE)* Look, why don't you come to my house for Christmas dinner. It'll be fun!

SCROOGE: Not going to happen.

FRED: Whatever. Have fun being miserable. *(starts acting like Scrooge behind his back; BOB laughs)* Merry Christmas, Bob!

BOB: Merry Christmas to you, Fred!

(FRED exits)

(PORTLY MAN #1 and PORTLY MAN #2 enter)

PORTLY MAN #1: Scrooge and Marley's, I believe. Have I the pleasure of addressing Mr. Scrooge, or Mr. Marley?

SCROOGE: Mr. Marley is dead. He died seven years ago, this very night.

PORTLY MAN #2: Bummer. We'll keep this short. You have a lot of money, and we want you to give some to the poor. You know, for food and stuff.

SCROOGE: *(to the audience)* Seriously? Give money to the poor? Who would THINK of such a thing! No way! *(very demanding)* Leave me alone and get out of my building!

(SCROOGE shoves PORTLY MEN out while they are giving dirty looks at SCROOGE)

SCROOGE: Time to go home, Bob. You'll want ALL day tomorrow, I suppose?

BOB: It IS Christmas, sir. Just saying.

SCROOGE: It IS ridiculous. And it's not fair. I have to pay you for NOT working and that makes me so mad! *(stomps up and down)*

BOB: Uh, sorry. Bye. *(to audience)* Wow, he has some real anger issues! I think he needs some counseling!

(BOB and SCROOGE exit opposite sides of stage)

ACT 1 SCENE 2

(enter SCROOGE with MARLEY'S GHOST wondering spookily around in the background, unseen by SCROOGE)

SCROOGE: *(muttering to himself)* I must be going crazy; I thought I saw old dead Marley's face on my door. Humbug! Oh well. Time for bed. *(he lies down on the floor and a bell starts ringing loudly, then there is the sound of loud footsteps offstage getting louder and louder)* It's humbug still! I won't believe it.

(enter MARLEY'S GHOST with a chain around his waist making moaning ghost like sounds)

MARLEY: What's up, Scroooooooooooge?!

SCROOGE: *(shocked)* Jacob Marley?!?! What do you want with me?

MARLEY: Ahhhhhhhhh!!! OOOOOOOOOO!!!!!! *(shakes chains)*

SCROOGE: *(screaming)* You're so scary! And you're dead! This is NOT happening!

MARLEY: *(to audience)* This is fun! *(to SCROOGE)* Yes, it IIIIIIIISSS happening. See this chain? SEEEEEEEEE IT??! Yeah, that's all the bad stuff I did when IIIIIIIIIIIII was alive. You should see youuuuuuuuur chain! It's a ponderous chain!

SCROOGE: Ponderous?

MARLEY: Yes, VERY, VEEEEEEEERY BIG!!!!

SCROOGE: Oh, that's not good. Old Jacob Marley, tell me more. Speak comfort to me, Jacob!

MARLEY: I have none to give. But listen up, pal. You don't have to turn out like me! Tonight you will be haunted by Three Spirits. You have to listen to them, okay? *(pauses waiting for an answer)* OKAY?! *(starts moaning and shaking chains)*

SCROOGE: *(really scared)* I'd rather not. *(MARLEY shakes chains dramatically at SCROOGE)* OKAY!

(MARLEY exits)

SCROOGE: Man, he was pushy! And I'm sure it's just my imagination acting up; ghosts aren't real. I'm going to bed!

(SCROOGE goes to sleep on stage)

ACT 2 SCENE 1

(enter GHOST OF CHRISTMAS PAST)

GHOST PAST: Ahem! *(waits a few seconds then starts waving his hands)* AHEM!!!!!!!!

SCROOGE: Aghhhhhh!!!! *(startled and jumps up off the floor)* Who, and what are you?

GHOST PAST: I am the Ghost of Christmas Past.

SCROOGE: *(to audience)* Aw, man, that Marley ghost was real! What a downer.

GHOST PAST: Look, we've got a lot of work to do and not much time, so let's go.

(GHOST PAST drags SCROOGE around the stage in a zig-zag)

SCROOGE: *(looking around, out of balance)* Wait a minute! I'm dizzy...hey, this is where I grew up. *(pointing at himself)* Hey, that's me!

(enter SCHOOL CHILDREN and YOUNG SCROOGE, laughing and playing tag; all of the children start picking on YOUNG SCROOGE; All SCHOOL CHILDREN run offstage leaving YOUNG SCROOGE onstage ...sad; he then follows them offstage)

GHOST PAST: *(laughing)* Whoa. That's harsh.

SCROOGE: *(really bummed)* They were so mean to me!

GHOST PAST: Kind of like the way you treat people today, right?

SCROOGE: But I was just a kid!

GHOST PAST: Yeah, stinks to be you. Come on, more to see... *(enter YOUNG SCROOGE and FAN; they hold hands and skip in a circle, looking happy)*

SCROOGE: *(really happy)* It's my sister! So young!

FAN: *(to YOUNG SCROOGE)* You're the best brother EVER!

GHOST PAST: Always a delicate creature, whom a breath might have withered. But she had a large heart.

SCROOGE: And now she's dead.

GHOST PAST: Dude, you're not going to get sad on me again, are you?

SCROOGE: *(glaring at GHOST PAST)* Humbug!

(YOUNG SCROOGE and FAN exit; enter FEZZIWIG)

SCROOGE: Why it's old Fezziwig. He was my boss when I was young, and look, he's alive again!

GHOST PAST: Right. That's kind of the whole point to this going back in time thing.

(SCROOGE shoots another glare at GHOST PAST)

FEZZIWIG: Let's dance! *(enter VILLAGERS and YOUNG SCROOGE; everyone starts clapping, laughing and dancing around FEZZIWIG who is acting like a conductor and waving his arms around)* Okay, listen up! *(everyone freezes)* It's time to go home, but I want everyone to have a super duper Merry Christmas. No excuses! *(ALL exit except YOUNG SCROOGE, SCROOGE and GHOST PAST)*

GHOST PAST: That Fezziwig was a cool guy. He made everyone feel so happy, didn't he?

SCROOGE: His power lies in words and looks. *(SCROOGE is deep in thought)*

GHOST PAST: What is the matter?

SCROOGE: *(turning away from GHOST PAST)* Nothing particular.

GHOST PAST: Something, I think? Come on.... Let it out... you can do it...

SCROOGE: No... *(mutters to himself)* Okay, maybe I should have been just a little nicer to Bob...

GHOST PAST: MAYBE?

(enter BELLE)

BELLE: *(really mad to YOUNG SCROOGE)* I'm totally breaking up with you because you used to love me, but now you just love money. *(throws money in the air, and SCROOGE starts running around grabbing it)* And you're mean! Hope you have a nice life, WITHOUT ME! See ya! *(she begins to exit)*

YOUNG SCROOGE: Wait, Belle, I do love money, but I love you! ...and....I love money....but, no...I love you too! *(sees more money on the ground)* But, the money.... *(starts picking up money; BELLE turns, does a final wave, and exits)*

YOUNG SCROOGE and SCROOGE: *(realizing Belle just left)* Nooooooo! *(YOUNG SCROOGE exits, and picks up more money on the way out)*

SCROOGE: Spirit! Why do you delight to torture me? No more! *(sees a dollar bill on the ground and picks it up)*

GHOST PAST: *(noticing SCROOGE)* Really? *(SCROOGE drops money)* Belle got married. You didn't. She had a family. You didn't. You missed out, man. Starting to get the picture?

SCROOGE: Yes, yes, yes!!! Now, make it stop!

GHOST PAST: Fine, fine. Let's go, you little crybaby. You should probably get some sleep.

SCROOGE: Sounds good to me.

(SCROOGE lies back on the floor and falls asleep; GHOST PAST tiptoes offstage)

(enter GHOST PRESENT wearing a robe and holding a turkey leg and a goblet)

GHOST PRESENT: Wake up, Scrooge! I am the Ghost of Christmas Present. Look upon me!

SCROOGE: I'm looking. Not that impressed. But let's get on with it.

GHOST PRESENT: Touch my robe! *(SCROOGE touches GHOST PRESENT's robe; pause; they look at each other)* Er...it must be broken. Guess we walk. Come on. *(they begin walking downstage)*

SCROOGE: Where are we going?

GHOST PRESENT: Your employee, Bob Cratchit's house. Oh look, here we are.

(enter BOB, MRS. CRATCHIT, PETER CRATCHIT, MARTHA CRATCHIT, TINY TIM, who has a crutch in one hand, and 3 other children; they are all holding bowls)

BOB: *(to audience)* Hi, we're the Cratchit family. We are a REALLY happy family!

MARTHA: *(to audience)* Yes, but we're REALLY poor, too. Thanks to HIS boss! *(pointing at BOB)*

PETER: *(to audience)* Yeah, as you can see our bowls are empty. *(shows empty bowl)* We practically survive off air.

TINY TIM: *(to audience)* But we're happy!

MRS. CRATCHIT: *(to audience; overly sappy)* Because we have each other.

TINY TIM: And love!

SCROOGE: *(to GHOST PRESENT)* Seriously, are they for real?

GHOST PRESENT: Yep! Adorable, isn't it?

BOB: A merry Christmas to us all.

TINY TIM: God bless us every one!

SCROOGE: Spirit, tell me if Tiny Tim will live.

GHOST PRESENT: *(puts hands to head as if looking into the future)* Ooooo, not so good....I see a vacant seat in the poor chimney corner, and a crutch without an owner. If SOMEBODY doesn't change SOMETHING, the child will die.

SCROOGE: No, no! Say he will be spared.

GHOST PRESENT: Nope, can't do that, sorry. Unless SOMEONE decides to change...hint, hint.

BOB: A Christmas toast to my boss, Mr. Scrooge! The founder of the feast!

MRS. CRATCHIT: *(angrily)* Oh sure, Mr. Scrooge! If he were here I'd give him a piece of my mind to feast upon. What an odious, stingy, hard, unfeeling man!

BOB: Dear, it's Christmas day. He's not THAT bad. *(Pause)* He's just... THAT sad. *(BOB holds up his bowl)* Come on, kids, to Scrooge!

PETER/MARTHA/TINY TIM: *(holding up their bowls)* To Scrooge!

PETER: *(muttering)* Thanks for nothing.

MRS. CRATCHIT: *(grabs his ear)* That's not nice.

MARTHA: And we Cratchits are ALWAYS nice. Read the book, Peter.

PETER: Sorry, Mom.

(the CRATCHIT FAMILY exits)

SCROOGE: She called me odious! Do I really smell that bad?

GHOST PRESENT: Odious doesn't mean you stink. Although in this case you do... according to the dictionary, odious means "unequivocally detestable." I mean, you are a toad sometimes Mr. Scrooge.

SCROOGE: Wow... that's kind of ... mean.

GHOST PRESENT: Wow, you are starting to get it; that's why the word "Scrooge" is associated with horrible people. Come on, we're not done. *(GHOST PRESENT and SCROOGE slowly walk across the stage; as they do, VILLAGERS appear onstage and sing a Christmas carol softly in the background)*

SCROOGE: *(moving around the people like they have some horrible virus or something)* These people are poor! And sick! Why are they singing? I don't understand where their happiness comes from. I don't understand anything anymore. I'm sooooo confused!!!

GHOST PRESENT: That's correct, you are confused. *(to audience)* This guy is truly a piece of work. *(to SCROOGE)* Okay, we're here.

(enter FRED and FRED'S WIFE; the VILLAGERS stop singing and gather around FRED)

FRED: *(laughs loudly while entering)* Ha, ha, ha! He said that Christmas was a Humbug. He believed it too! *(everyone laughs)*

FRED'S WIFE: More shame for him, Fred.

FRED: Well, he's not very nice. I mean, some might even call him... odious!

SCROOGE: *(to GHOST PRESENT)* They're talking about me, aren't they?

GHOST PRESENT: What gave it away, the humbug or the odious comment? *(SCROOGE makes a face at GHOST PRESENT)*

FRED'S WIFE: But he's SUPER rich! Seriously, I mean a LOT of money!

FRED: So what? He don't do any good with it. He don't make himself comfortable with it. But I am sorry for him. He's only making himself miserable, not us! Ha! Poor old Scrooge. But, he is fun to laugh at!

FRED'S WIFE: I know, let's play a game. How 'bout YES and NO? You go first, Fred.

FRED: Okay! *(the VILLAGERS and FRED'S WIFE gather to one side of FRED)*

VILLAGER #1: Are you an animal?

FRED: Yes!

VILLAGER #2: Are you a bear?

FRED: No.

VILLAGER #3: A cat?

FRED: No.

VILLAGER #4: A cow, no wait, a pig?

FRED: No! *(starts stomping around the stage making frightening animal noises; everyone starts laughing)*

FRED'S WIFE: I know what it is, Fred! It's your uncle Scro-o-o-o-oge!

FRED: Yes! *(everyone laughs more, even SCROOGE laughs a little)* He deserves a toast. To Uncle Scrooge!

VILLAGERS/FRED'S WIFE: *(everyone raises their hands to toast)* Uncle Scrooge! *(FRED, FRED'S WIFE and VILLAGERS exit)*

SCROOGE: *(to GHOST PRESENT)* I don't know whether to laugh or cry.

GHOST PRESENT: It will take a lot of laughter AND a lot of tears to unfreeze that cold heart of yours. I'd get to it if I were you, this play's almost over, and I'm done here. Later 'gator.

(GHOST PRESENT taps SCROOGE on the head and SCROOGE falls immediately asleep; GHOST PRESENT exits)

ACT 3 SCENE 1

(Enter GHOST OF CHRISTMAS YET TO COME dressed in a black gown acting all ghostly-like; shakes SCROOGE vigorously)

SCROOGE: *(wakes up startled)* Who goes there! *(sees GHOST who waves at SCROOGE)* Let me guess. You're the Ghost of Christmas Yet to Come?

(GHOST YET TO COME gives him two thumbs up)

SCROOGE: Not a big talker, are ya?

(GHOST YET TO COME shakes his head "no" and points to two VILLAGERS who have entered upstage; GHOST YET TO COME shoves SCROOGE towards the VILLAGERS)

VILLAGER #1: I don't know much about it. I only know he's dead.

VILLAGER #2: What did he do with his money?

VILLAGER #1: Who knows. He didn't leave it to me. *(VILLAGERS laugh)*

VILLAGER #2: Well you know no one will be at HIS funeral. And I heard that some poor people went through his house and took a bunch of his stuff after he died. He didn't have any family or friends there to stop them. He died sad and alone.

VILLAGER #1: Nobody liked him anyway. I hear he was odious! Good riddance, I say! *(VILLAGERS exit)*

SCROOGE: Hmmmm. That's awful. I'd hate to be THAT person, because I know what odious means now...I wonder who they're talking about.

(GHOST YET TO COME shakes head dramatically and points to the other side of the stage where BOB, MRS. CRATCHIT, MARTHA CRATCHIT, and PETER CRATCHIT enter)

MARTHA: *(to audience)* Our Tiny Tim is gone.

PETER: *(to audience)* Dead.

BOB: *(melodramatically crying)* My little, little child!

MRS. CRATCHIT: *(crying)* His new home is in the ground. If only we had just a LITTLE money, we could have saved him! *(she looks over at SCROOGE)*

SCROOGE: *(taken aback; to GHOST YET TO COME)* Hey, can she see me? *(GHOST YET TO COME shakes his head, "no")* This is so depressing; this is supposed to be a comedy! *(to GHOST YET TO COME)* Can't we skip this part?

(GHOST YET TO COME shakes head "no")

SCROOGE: Yeah, I didn't think so.

BOB: None of us must ever forget our dear Tiny Tim!

MARTHA and PETER: Never, father!

BOB: That makes me happy.

(CRATCHITS exit)

SCROOGE: This is an awful future. I don't like it at all! Can't we stop this?

GHOST YET TO COME: *(frustrated)* NO!

SCROOGE: *(shocked)* HEY! Wait a minute, I thought you couldn't talk!

GHOST YET TO COME: Yeah, well, you just weren't getting the point, were you?!?! *(to audience)* I'm usually so spooky!!!

SCROOGE: Okay, what's next? Lay it on me; I can take it!

(GHOST YET TO COME nods and claps hands; when nothing happens he claps his hands again; a VILLAGER runs onstage, places a cardboard headstone down and runs offstage)

SCROOGE: What's that? *(he runs to headstone and picks it up; it says "EBENEZER SCROOGE" in big letters)* Noooooooooo!!! Am I the sad, pathetic, odious, DEAD man they were talking about earlier?

EVERYONE BACKSTAGE: YES!!!

(GHOST YET TO COME nods head and gives him two thumbs up)

SCROOGE: Oh no, no! I can change! I will honor Christmas in my heart, and try to keep it all the year. I will live in the Past, the Present, and the Future. I will not shut out the lessons they teach. Please! Pretty, pretty please! Give me a chance. *(SCROOGE starts crying melodramatically and throws himself on the floor like he's five and having a tantrum)*

(GHOST YET TO COME pats SCROOGE on the back and then raises arms up in the air like a champion who just won a game; he gives SCROOGE a big thumbs up, waves "bye" at audience and then exits)

SCROOGE: *(stops crying and looks around)* Why, I'm home! It's my bed and my room! I am as light as a feather, I am as happy as an angel, I am as merry as a schoolboy. A merry Christmas to everybody! *(points to some random audience member)* Even you, random audience member! A happy New Year to all the world. *(he starts laughing like a crazy person and skips around the stage; a VILLAGER enters)*

SCROOGE: Hey you! What's today?

VILLAGER: Um, seriously? Why, it's Christmas Day.

SCROOGE: Woooo-hooooo!

VILLAGER: *(VILLAGER thinks he's crazy)* Yeah...woo-hoo. *(VILLAGER starts to exit)*

SCROOGE: Wait! If I give you some money, will you do me a favor? Go buy the biggest turkey you can find and take it to the Cratchit family. *(SCROOGE gives VILLAGER some money)*

VILLAGER: Really? Consider it done. Thanks! *(VILLAGER exits; enter PORTLY MAN #1)*

SCROOGE: Oh! It's you! Do you still need money for poor people? 'Cause I want to give you a whole bunch!

PORTLY MAN #1: My dear Mr. Scrooge, are you serious or just humbugging me?

SCROOGE: As serious as chocolate cake!

PORTLY MAN #1: Wow, chocolate cake IS serious stuff. *(a large bag of cash is thrown onstage; SCROOGE picks it up and tosses it to PORTLY MAN)*

SCROOGE: Here!

PORTLY MAN #1: Sweet! Thanks Scrooge!

(PORTLY MAN #1 exits; FRED and FRED'S WIFE enter)

SCROOGE: Fred! And Fred's wife! What is your name, anyway? Dickens really dropped the ball there. Anyway, I have come to dinner! It'll be fun!

FRED: Fun?!?! Wow! How unbelievably awesome! If you weren't standing in front of me, I wouldn't believe you're my uncle! *(they laugh)*

FRED'S WIFE: Let's go eat!

(ALL exit)

ACT 3 SCENE 3

(enter BOB and SCROOGE from opposite sides of the stage)

SCROOGE: *(VERY serious)* You're late, Bob!

BOB: *(his head bowed down doesn't see SCROOGE smile and laugh at audience)* I am very sorry, sir.

SCROOGE: You better be! *(giggles to the audience like a kid)* I am not going to stand this sort of thing any longer. And therefore...(SCROOGE raises his arm as though he's going to hit BOB) I am about to raise your salary!

BOB: Say what?!?!

SCROOGE: HA! Didn't see that coming, did you? *(SCROOGE starts doing some type of money dance, while giggling to himself)*

BOB: *(shocked)* Who are you, and what have you done with Mr. Scrooge?

SCROOGE: A merry Christmas, Bob! I'm going to give you more money, I'm going to help your family, and I'm going to be a good person from now on. Isn't that great?

BOB: I can't believe it! This is totally weird, but so cool!

SCROOGE: Right?

(TINY TIM enters)

TINY TIM: God bless us, every one!

(ALL exit)

THE END

Sneak Peeks at other Playing With Plays books:

The Jungle Book for Kids

PARENT WOLF: Oh hi, Bagheera. What's happening in the life of a panther?

BAGHEERA: I wanted to warn you. Shere Khan's in town again.

PARENT WOLF: The tiger? What's he doing in this part of the jungle?

BAGHEERA: What tigers do. You know, hunt, eat, hunt again, eat... hunt...eat... *(trailing off)*

PARENT WOLF: *(play-acting like a tiger)* Oh look at me, I'm a mean ol' tiger, roar!!! *(there is a LOUD ROAR and GROWL from offstage, PARENT WOLF is a bit shocked)*

BAGHEERA: Listen! That's him now!

(enter MOWGLI, running off-balance, and falling down)

PARENT WOLF: Whoa! A man's cub! Look! *(ALL turn to look at MOWGLI)* How little and so... smelly, but cute! *(starts petting his hair)*

(BAGHEERA sneaks over to MOWGLI and whispers something in his ear. MOWGLI sighs and gets down on his knees to appear smaller; he remains on his knees throughout the rest of the scene and ACT1 SCENE 2)

MOWGLI: *(very sarcastically)* Gaa gaa. Goo goo.

(SHERE KHAN enters; paRENT WOLF hides MOWGLI behind her back)

SHERE KHAN: A man's cub went this way. Its parents have run off. Give it to me. I'll uh... take care of him... *(as he rubs his belly)* you can TOTALLY trust me! *(gives* *the audience a big evil smile)*

PARENT WOLF: You are NOT the boss of us.

SHERE KHAN: Excuse me?! Do you know who I am? It is I, Shere Khan, who speaks! I'm kind of a big deal. And scary! GRRRRR.

PARENT WOLF: The man's cub is mine; he shall not be killed! So beat it; you don't scare us.

SHERE KHAN: Fine. But I'll get him some day, make no mistake! Muahahahahaha! ROAR! *(SHERE KHAN exits)*

PARENT WOLF: *(to MOWGLI)* Mowgli the Frog I will call thee. Lie still, little frog.

MOWGLI: *(to PARENT WOLF)* Frog?

PARENT WOLF: *(to MOWGLI and audience)* Yeah, I guess Rudyard Kipling liked frogs! But now we have to see what the wolf leader says.

(enter AKELA, BAGHEERA, and BALOO)

AKELA: Okay, wolves, let's get this meeting started! Howl!

WOLVES: Howl!! *(ALL WOLVES howl)*

PARENT WOLF: Akela, our great leader, I'd like to present the newest member of our pack, Mowgli the Frog!

AKELA: Hmmm, Frog, huh? If you say so.

(enter SHERE KHAN)

SHERE KHAN: ROAR! The cub is mine! Give him to me!

AKELA: Who speaks for this cub?

BALOO: *(speaking in a big, deep bear voice!)* I, Baloo the Bear, I speak for the man's cub. I myself will teach him the ways of the jungle.

Two Gentlemen of Verona for Kids

ANTONIO: It's not nothing.

PROTEUS: Ahhhhh......It's a letter from Valentine, telling me what a great time he's having in Milan, yeah... that's what it says!

ANTONIO: Awesome! Glad to hear it! Because, you leave tomorrow to join Valentine in Milan.

PROTEUS: What!? Dad! No way! I don't want... I mean, I need some time. I've got some things to do.

ANTONIO: Like what?

PROTEUS: You know...things! Important things! And stuff! Lots of stuff!

ANTONIO: No more excuses! Go pack your bag. *(ANTONIO begins to exit)*

PROTEUS: Fie!

ANTONIO: What was that?

PROTEUS: Fiiii......ne with me, Pops! *(ANTONIO exits)* I was afraid to show my father Julia's letter, lest he should take exceptions to my love; and my own lie of an excuse made it easier for him to send me away.

ANTONIO: *(Offstage)* Proteus! Get a move on!!

PROTEUS: Fie!!!

(exit)

ACT 2 SCENE 1

(enter VALENTINE and SPEED following)

VALENTINE: Ah, Silvia, Silvia! *(heavy sighs)*

SPEED: *(mocking)* Madam Silvia! Madam Silvia! Gag me.

VALENTINE: Knock it off! You don't know her.

SPEED: Do too. She's the one that you can't stop staring at. Makes me wanna barf.

VALENTINE: I do not stare!

SPEED: You do. AND you keep singing that silly love song. *(sing INSERT SAPPY LOVE SONG)* You used to be so much fun.

VALENTINE: Huh? *(heavy sigh, starts humming SAME LOVE SONG)*

SPEED: Never mind.

VALENTINE: I have loved her ever since I saw her. Here she comes!

SPEED: Great. *(to audience)* Watch him turn into a fool.

(enter SILVIA)

VALENTINE: Hey, Silvia.

SILVIA: Hey, Valentine. What's goin' on?

VALENTINE: Nothin'. What's goin' on with you?

SILVIA: Nothin'.

(pause)

VALENTINE: What are you doing later?

SILVIA: Not sure. Prob-ly nothin'. You?

VALENTINE: Me neither. Nothin'.

SILVIA: Yea?

VALENTINE: Probably.

SPEED: *(to audience)* Kill me now.

SILVIA: Well, I guess I better go.

VALENTINE: Oh, okay! See ya'..

(pause)

SILVIA: See ya' later maybe?

VALENTINE: Oh, yea! Maybe! Yea! Okay!

SILVIA: Bye.

VALENTINE: Bye!

(exit SILVIA)

SPEED: *(aside)* Wow. *(to VALENTINE)* Dude, what the heck was that?

VALENTINE: I think she has a boyfriend. I can tell.

SPEED: Dude! She is so into you! How could you not see that?

VALENTINE: Do you think?

SPEED: Come on. We'll talk it through over dinner. *(to audience)* Fool. Am I right?

(exit)

The Tempest for Kids

PROSPERO: Hast thou, spirit, performed to point the tempest that I bade thee?

ARIEL: What? Was that English?

PROSPERO: *(Frustrated)* Did you make the storm hit the ship?

ARIEL: Why didn't you say that in the first place? Oh yeah! I rocked that ship! They didn't know what hit them.

PROSPERO: Why, that's my spirit! But are they, Ariel, safe?

ARIEL: Not a hair perished.

PROSPERO: Woo-hoo! All right. We've got more work to do.

ARIEL: Wait a minute. You're still going to free me, right, Master?

PROSPERO: Oh, I see. Is it sooooo terrible working for me? Huh? Remember when I saved you from that witch? Do you? Remember when that blue-eyed hag locked you up and left you for dead? Who saved you? Me, that's who!

ARIEL: I thank thee, master.

PROSPERO: I will free you in two days, okay? Sheesh. Patience is a virtue, or haven't you heard. Right. Where was I? Oh yeah... I need you to disguise yourself like a sea nymph and then... *(PROSPERO whispers something in ARIEL'S ear)* Got it?

ARIEL: Got it. *(ARIEL exits)*

PROSPERO: *(to MIRANDA)* Awake, dear heart, awake!

(MIRANDA yawns loudly)

PROSPERO: Shake it off. Come on. We'll visit Caliban, my slave.

MIRANDA: The witch's son? You mean the MONSTER! He's creepy and stinky!!!

PROSPERO: Mysterious and sneaky,

MIRANDA: Altogether freaky,

MIRANDA & PROSPERO: He's Caliban the slave!!! *(snap, snap!)*

PROSPERO: *(Calls offstage)* What, ho! Slave! Caliban!

(enter CALIBAN)

CALIBAN: Oh, look it's the island stealers! This is my home! My mother, the witch, left it to me and now you treat me like dirt.

MIRANDA: Oh boo-hoo! I used to feel sorry for you, I even taught you our language, but you tried to hurt me so now we have to lock you in that cave.

CALIBAN: I wish I had never learned your language!

PROSPERO: Go get us wood! If you don't, I'll rack thee with old cramps, and fill all thy bones with aches!

CALIBAN: *(to AUDIENCE)* He's so mean to me! But I have to do what he says. ANNOYING! *(exit CALIBAN)*

(enter FERDINAND led by "invisible" ARIEL)

ARIEL: *(Singing)* Who let the dogs out?! Woof, woof, woof!! *(Spookily)* The watchdogs bark; bow-wow, bow-wow!

FERDINAND: *(Dancing across stage)* Where should this music be? Where is it taking me! What's going on?

Hamlet for Kids

(enter GERTRUDE and POLONIUS)

GERTRUDE: What's up, Polonius?

POLONIUS: I am going to hide and spy on your conversation with Hamlet!

GERTRUDE: Oh, okay.

(POLONIUS hides somewhere, enter HAMLET very mad, swinging his sword around)

HAMLET: MOM!!! I AM VERY MAD!

GERTRUDE: Ahhh! You scared me!

(POLONIUS sneezes from hiding spot)

HAMLET: *(not seeing POLONIUS)* How now, a rat? Who's hiding? *(stabs POLONIUS)*

POLONIUS: O, I am slain! Ohhhh the pain! *(dies on stage)*

GERTRUDE: Oh me, what has thou done?

HAMLET: Oops, I thought that was Claudius. Hmph, oh well... as I was saying, I AM MAD you married uncle Claudius!

GERTRUDE: Oh that, yeah, sorry. *(in a motherly voice)* Now, you just killed Polonius, clean up this mess and go to your room!

HAMLET: Okay Mom.

(all exit)

ACT 4 SCENES 1-3

(enter GERTRUDE and CLAUDIUS)

GERTRUDE: Ahhh, Dear?

CLAUDIUS: Yeah?

GERTRUDE: Ummmm, you would not believe what I have seen tonight! Polonius is dead.

CLAUDIUS: WHAT!?

GERTRUDE: Yeah, Hamlet was acting a little crazy, Polonius sneezed or something, then Hamlet yelled, "A rat, a rat!" and then WHACK! It was over.

CLAUDIUS: *(very angry)* HAMLET!!!! GET OVER HERE NOW!!!!!

(enter HAMLET)

CLAUDIUS: *(very casual)* Hey, what's up?

HAMLET: What noise, who calls on Hamlet? What do you want?

CLAUDIUS: Now, Hamlet. Where's Polonius' body?

HAMLET: I'm not telling!

CLAUDIUS: Oh come on, please tell me!!! Please! With a cherry on top! Where is Polonius?

HAMLET: Oh, all right. He's over there, up the stairs into the lobby. *(points offstage)*

(POLONIUS enters and dies again)

CLAUDIUS: Ewe... he's a mess! Hamlet, I am sending you off to England.

HAMLET: Fine! Farewell, dear Mother. And I'm taking this with me! *(HAMLET takes POLONIUS offstage)*

(all exit but CLAUDIUS)

CLAUDIUS: *(to audience)* I have arranged his execution in England! *(laughs evilly as he exits)* Muwahahaha...

Taming of the Shrew for Kids

ACT 1 SCENE 1

(Enter LUCENTIO and TRANIO)

LUCENTIO: Well, Tranio, my trusty servant, here we are in Padua, Italy! I can't wait to start studying and learn all about philosophy and virtue!

TRANIO: There is such a thing as too much studying, master Lucentio. We need to remember to have fun too! PARTY!

LUCENTIO: Hey look! Here come some of the locals!

(LUCENTIO and TRANIO move to side of stage; Enter BAPTISTA, KATHERINA, BIANCA, HORTENSIO and GREMIO)

BAPTISTA: Look guys, you know the rules: Bianca can't marry anybody until her older sister, Katherina, is married. That's the plan and I'm sticking to it! If either of you both love Katherina, then please, take her.

KATHERINA: *(Sarcastically)* Wow, thanks Dad.

HORTENSIO: I wouldn't marry her if she were the last woman on earth.

KATHERINA: And I'd rather scratch your face off than marry you!

TRANIO: *(Aside to LUCENTIO)* That wench is stark mad!

BAPTISTA: Enough of this! Bianca, go inside.

BIANCA: Yes, dearest father. My books and

instruments shall be my company. *(She exits)*

KATHERINA: *(At BIANCA)* Goody two-shoes.

BAPTISTA: Bianca is so talented in music, instruments, and poetry! I really need to hire some tutors for her. *(KATHERINA rolls her eyes and sighs)* Good-day everyone! *(BAPTISTA exits)*

KATHERINA: *(Very angry)* AGHHHH!!!! I'm outta here

(Exits opposite direction from her father)

GREMIO: *(Shudders)* Ugh! How could anyone ever want to marry Katherina?!

HORTENSIO: I don't know, but let's find a husband for her.

GREMIO: A husband? A devil!

HORTENSIO: I say a husband.

GREMIO: I say a devil.

HORTENSIO: Alright, alright! There's got to be a guy out there crazy enough to marry her.

GREMIO: Let's get to it!

(Exit GREMIO and HORTENSIO)

LUCENTIO: Oh, Tranio! Sweet Bianca, has stolen my heart! I burn, I pine, I perish! Oh, how I love her!

TRANIO: Whoa, Master! You're getting a little over dramatic, there, Lucentio.

LUCENTIO: Sorry. But my heart is seriously on fire! How am I going to make her fall in love with me if she's not allowed to date anybody? Hmmm...

TRANIO: What if you pretended to be a tutor and went to teach her?

PlayingWithPlays.com

LUCENTIO: YOU ARE BRILLIANT, TRANIO! And because we're new here and no one knows what we look like yet, YOU will pretend to be ME at all the local parties. Quick, let's change clothes.

TRANIO: Here? Now?

LUCENTIO: Yes, Here and now! You can't stop this lovin' feeling! *(Starts singing a love song)*

TRANIO: Please, no singing. I'll do it. *(They exchange hats, socks or jackets)*

Oliver Twist
for Kids

(enter FAGIN, SIKES, DODGER and NANCY)

DODGER: So that Oliver kid got caught by the police.

FAGIN: He could tell them all our secrets and get us in trouble; we've got to find him. Like, in the next 30 seconds or so.

SIKES: Send Nancy. She's good at getting information quick.

NANCY: Nope. Don't wanna go, Sikes. I like the kid.

SIKES: She'll go, Fagin.

NANCY: No, she won't, Fagin.

SIKES: Yes, she will, Fagin.

NANCY: Fine! Grrrrr....

(NANCY sticks out her tongue at SIKES and storms offstage, then immediately returns)

NANCY: Okay, I checked with my sources and, some gentleman took him home to take care of him.

(NANCY, DODGER and SIKES stare at FAGIN waiting for direction)

FAGIN: Where?

NANCY: I don't know.

FAGIN: WHAT!?!? *(waiting)* Well don't just stand there, GO FIND HIM! *(to audience)* Can't find any good help these days!

(all run offstage, bumping into each other in their haste)

ACT 2 SCENE 2

(enter OLIVER)

OLIVER: *(to audience)* I'm out running an errand for Mr. Brownlow to prove that I'm a trustworthy boy. I can't keep hanging out with thieves, right?

(enter NANCY, who runs over to OLIVER and grabs him; SIKES, FAGIN, and DODGER enter shortly after and follow NANCY)

NANCY: Oh my dear brother! I've found him! Oh! Oliver! Oliver!

OLIVER: What!?!? I don't have a sister!

NANCY: You do now, kid. Let's go. *(she drags OLIVER to FAGIN)*

FAGIN: Dodger, take Oliver and lock him up.

DODGER: *(to OLIVER)* Sorry, dude. *(DODGER and OLIVER start to exit)*

OLIVER: Aw, man! Seriously? I just found a good home...

NANCY: Don't be too mean to him, Fagin.

OLIVER: *(as he's exiting)* Yeah, don't be too mean to me, Fagin!

SIKES: *(mimicking NANCY)* Don't be mean, Fagin. Wah, wah, wah. Look, I need Oliver to help me rob a house, okay? He is just the size I want to fit through the window. All sneaky ninja like.

Much Ado About Nothing
for Kids

ACT 1 SCENE 1

(Enter LEONATO, HERO, and BEATRICE)

LEONATO: *(to audience)* I am The Governor. Governor of Messina, Italy.

HERO: Whatever, Dad. You are always talking about yourself. We know you're "The Governor". We've got it. *(sarcastically)* Governor Leonato.

LEONATO: Now listen to me, Hero. You need to behave yourself. We have guests coming. *(BEATRICE laughs at Hero)* And you Beatrice, you better watch your tongue, because I don't want you getting into a "war of words" with Benedick, again. Got me? Look, here comes a messenger.

(enter MESSENGER)

MESSENGER: Sir, I come to tell you that Don Pedro, the Prince of Arragon, his brother Don John, and his faithful men, Claudio and Benedick, will all be coming soon.

(exit MESSENGER)

HERO: Oh, goodie! I think Claudio is cute!

BEATRICE: Yeah, well, Benedick is NOT! He's always smelly after a battle! Oh look, here comes the smelly one now.

(enter DON JOHN, DON PEDRO, BENEDICK, and CLAUDIO)

LEONATO: Welcome, Don Pedro and friends! You have fought bravely. Please stay and party with us.

DON PEDRO: We will, thank you!

DON JOHN: *(aside and pouting to the audience)* My brother gets all the attention! I hate him!

DON PEDRO: Don John, what are you saying over there?

DON JOHN: Oh nothing, dear brother. *(starts dancing VERY badly)* Just practicing my dance moves for the party!

BEATRICE: *(mockingly to BENEDICK)* So Benedick, you're back again? *(sniffs him)* And, whew! *(plugging her nose with her fingers)* Smelly as usual.

BENEDICK: *(mockingly in a high girl's voice)* "Smelly as usual." You, my dear Beatrice, are a pain as usual. Are you ready to continue our merry war?

BEATRICE: You mean our war of words? You know it!

BENEDICK: You are such a parrot-teacher.

BEATRICE: What did you call me?

BENEDICK: Someone who talks A LOT! What's the matter? Forget your dictionary? You know, *(said slowly as if she doesn't understand English)* PARROT TEACHER.

BEATRICE: Humph! A bird of my tongue is better than a beast of yours!

BENEDICK: I wish my horse had the speed of your tongue!

BEATRICE: *(to audience)* Oh, he makes me sooooo mad! *(BEATRICE stomps her feet like a 4-year old and storms offstage)*

LEONATO: *(to audience)* There's a skirmish of wit between them. *(to all)* Everyone, let's go to my castle.

You know, the castle that belongs to The Governor? *(with two thumbs pointing at himself)*

(all exit except CLAUDIO and BENEDICK)

CLAUDIO: *(to BENEDICK)* Hero is sooooooo cute!

BENEDICK: Whoa, did you just say, "cute"? No, no, no, NO! A kitten is cute, a baby is cute, but her? No. With a name like "Hero", she can NOT be cute!

CLAUDIO: Yeah, what about her name?

BENEDICK: Come on. "Hero?" Does she drive the Batmobile and wear a cape, too?

CLAUDIO: Leave her alone because...because...because I think I want to marry her!

BENEDICK: Marry? Whoa, buddy! Listen, I mean, she's a bit..... plain. Actually, I do not like her. And as for marriage, it's overrated, so last year. You'll never catch me getting married. That's right, the single life for me!

CLAUDIO: *(CLAUDIO is day dreamy and lovesick)* She is the sweetest lady that I ever looked on. Could you buy such a jewel?

BENEDICK: *(to audience)* And a case to put her into.

(enter DON PEDRO)

DON PEDRO: Where have you guys been?

BENEDICK: You won't believe this! Lovesick Claudio here wants to marry Hero. Hah! Isn't that hilarious!?

DON PEDRO: Be careful Benedick, my friend. Remember, this is a comedy, and all of Shakespeare's comedies end in marriage.

CLAUDIO: Yeah!

PlayingWithPlays.com

The Three Musketeers for Kids

(ATHOS and D'ARTAGNAN enter)

ATHOS: Glad you could make it. I have engaged two of my friends as seconds.

D'ARTAGNAN: Seconds?

ATHOS: Yeah, they make sure we fight fair. Oh, here they are now!

(enter ARAMIS and PORTHOS singing, "Bad boys, bad boys, watcha gonna do...")

PORTHOS: Hey! I'm fighting him in an hour. I am going to fight... because...well... I am going to fight!

ARAMIS: And I fight him at two o'clock! Ours is a theological quarrel. *(does a thinking pose)*

D'ARTAGNAN: Yeah, yeah, yeah... I'll get to you soon!

ATHOS: We are the Three Musketeers; Athos, Porthos, and Aramis.

D'ARTAGNAN: Whatever, Ethos, Pathos, and Logos, let's just finish this! *(swords crossed and are about to fight; enter JUSSAC and cardinal's guards)*

PORTHOS: The cardinal's guards! Sheathe your swords, gentlemen.

JUSSAC: Dueling is illegal! You are under arrest!

ARAMIS: *(to ATHOS and PORTHOS)* There are five of them and we are but three.

D'ARTAGNAN: *(steps forward to join them)* It appears to me we are four! I have the spirit; my heart is that of a Musketeer.

PORTHOS: Great! I love fighting!

(Musketeers say "Fight, fight fight!...Fight, fight, fight!" as they are fighting; D'ARTAGNAN fights JUSSAC and it's the big fight; JUSSAC is wounded and exits; the 3 MUSKETEERS cheer)

ATHOS: Well done! Let's go see Treville and the king!

ARAMIS: And we don't have to kill you now!

PORTHOS: And let's get some food, too! I'm hungry!

D'ARTAGNAN: *(to audience)* This is fun!

(ALL exit)

ACT 2 SCENE 1

(enter 3 MUSKETEERS, D'ARTAGNAN, and TREVILLE)

TREVILLE: The king wants to see you, and he's not too happy you killed a few of the cardinal's guards.

(enter KING)

KING: *(yelling)* YOU GUYS HUMILIATED THE CARDINAL'S GUARDS!

ATHOS: Sire, they attacked us!

KING: Oh...Well then, bravo! I hear D'Artagnan beat the cardinal's best swordsman! Brave young man! Here's some money for you. Enjoy! *(hands money to D'ARTAGNAN)*

D'ARTAGNAN: Sweet!

(ALL exit)

Sneak peek of
Henry V for Kids

ACT 2 SCENE 2

(enter BEDFORD and EXETER, observing CAMBRIDGE and SCROOP, who whisper among themselves)

BEDFORD: Hey Exeter, do you think it's a good idea that King Henry is letting those conspirators wander around freely?

EXETER: It's alright, Bedford. King Henry has a plan! He knows EVERYTHING they are plotting. BUT, they don't KNOW he knows. And HE knows that they don't know he knows...and...

BEDFORD: *(interrupting)* Okay, okay, I get it. Let's go sit in the audience and watch! *(they sit in the audience; enter HENRY)*

HENRY: Greetings, my good and FAITHFUL friends, Cambridge and Scroop. Perfect timing! I need your advice on something.

CAMBRIDGE: Sure thing. You know we'd do anything for you! Never was a monarch better feared and loved.

SCROOP: That's why we're going to kick some French butt!! *(SCROOP and CAMBRIDGE high-five)*

HENRY: Excellent! A man was arrested yesterday for shouting nasty things about me. But I'm sure by now he's thought better of it. I think I ought to show mercy and pardon him.

SCROOP: Nah, let him be punished.

HENRY: Ahhh, but let us yet be merciful.

CAMBRIDGE: Nah, I'm with Scroop! Off with his head!

HENRY: Is that your final answer?

CAMBRIDGE & SCROOP: YES!

HENRY: Ok, but if we don't show mercy for small offenses, how will we show mercy for big ones? I will release him. Now, take a look at THESE LETTERS.

(as CAMBRIDGE and SCROOP read the letters, their jaws drop)

HENRY: Why, how now, gentlemen? What see you in those papers that your jaws hang so low?

EXETER: *(to audience)* The letters betray their guilt!

CAMBRIDGE: I do confess my fault...

SCROOP:....and do submit me to your Highness' mercy! *(they start begging and pleading on the ground)*

HENRY: Exeter, Bedford, arrest these traitors. What did they say... Oh yeah, OFF WITH THEIR HEADS!

CAMBRIDGE: Whoa there!

SCROOP: Off with our what? What happened to the whole "mercy" thing you were just talking about!?

HENRY: Your own words talked me out of it! Take them away!

CAMBRIDGE: Well, this stinks!

(EXETER and BEDFORD arrest CAMBRIDGE and SCROOP; ALL exit, except HENRY)

HENRY: Being king is no fun sometimes. Scroop used to be one of my best friends. *(SCROOP runs on stage and dies melodramatically)* But there's no time to mope! *(CAMBRIDGE runs on stage and dies on top of SCROOP)* The signs of war advance. No king of England, if not King of France! NOW CLEAN UP THIS MESS!

(ALL exit)

Richard III for Kids

ACT 1 SCENE 4

(CLARENCE is in prison, sleeping; he wakes up from a bad dream)

CLARENCE: Terrible, horrible, no good, very bad dream! *(pauses, notices audience and addresses them)* O, I have pass'd a miserable night! I dreamt that Richard was trying to kill me! Hahahaha, Richard is SUCH a good guy, he would NEVER do a thing like that!

(enter MURDERER carrying a weapon)

MURDERER: I sounded like such a pro, no one will know it's my first day on the job! Hehehe!

CLARENCE: Hey! Who's there?

MURDERER: Um... um... *(hides his murder weapon behind his back)*

CLARENCE: Your eyes do menace me. Are you planning to murder me? 'Cause that's not a good idea. My brother Richard is a REALLY powerful guy.

MURDERER: Ha! Richard is the one who sent me here to do this! *(a pause)* Whoops...

CLARENCE: Hahaha, you foolish fellow. Richard loves me.

MURDERER: Dude, what are you not getting? He PAID me to do this!

CLARENCE: O, do not slander him, for he is kind.

(The MURDERER stabs CLARENCE. CLARENCE dies a dramatic death)

CLARENCE: Kinda ruthless... *(dies)*

MURDERER: *(Gasps)* Oh, my! He's dead! I feel bad now... I bet Clarence was a really nice guy. Ahhh, the guilt! Wow, I should have stayed in clown school.

(MURDERER exits)

ACT 2 SCENE 1

(KING EDWARD is surrounded by QUEEN ELIZABETH and BUCKINGHAM)

KING EDWARD: Well, this has been a great day at work! Everyone's agreed to get along!

(ELIZABETH and BUCKINGHAM shake hands with each other to celebrate the peace. Enter RICHARD. KING EDWARD smiles happily)

KING EDWARD: If I die, I will be at peace! But I must say I'm feeling a lot healthier after all of this peace-making!

RICHARD: Hey! Looks like you're all in a good mood. That's great, 'cause you know I LOVE getting along! So what's up?

KING EDWARD: I made them like each other!

RICHARD: How lovely! I like you all now, too! Group hug? *(everyone shakes their head)* No? *(he grins sweetly)*

ELIZABETH: Wonderful! Once Clarence gets back from the Tower, everything will be perfect!

RICHARD: WHAT??? We make peace and then you insult us like this? That's no way to talk about a DEAD man!!

(EVERYONE gasps)

KING EDWARD: Is Clarence dead? I told them to cancel the execution!

RICHARD: Oh, yeah... guess that was too late! *(winks to audience)*

KING EDWARD: Nooooooo!!!! Oh my poor brother! Now I feel more sick than EVER! Oh, poor Clarence!

(All exit except RICHARD and BUCKINGHAM)

RICHARD: Well, that sure worked as planned!

BUCKINGHAM: Great job, partner!

(both exit, laughing evilly)

Treasure Island
for Kids

(enter JIM, TRELAWNEY, and DOCTOR; enter CAPTAIN SMOLLETT from the other side of the stage)

TRELAWNEY: Hello Captain. Are we all shipshape and seaworthy?

CAPTAIN: Trelawney, I don't know what you're thinking, but I don't like this cruise; and I don't like the men.

TRELAWNEY: *(very angry)* Perhaps you don't like the ship?

CAPTAIN: Nope, I said it short and sweet.

DOCTOR: What? Why?

CAPTAIN: Because I heard we are going on a treasure hunt and the coordinates of the island are: *(whispers to DOCTOR)*

DOCTOR: Wow! That's exactly right!

CAPTAIN: There's been too much blabbing already.

DOCTOR: Right! But, I doubt ANYTHING will go wrong!

CAPTAIN: Fine. Let's sail!

(ALL exit)

Act 2 Scene 3

(enter JIM, SILVER, and various other pirates)

SILVER: Ay, ay, mates. You know the song: Fifteen men on the dead man's chest.

ALL PIRATES: Yo-ho-ho and a bottle of rum!

(PIRATES slowly exit)

JIM: *(to the audience)* So, the Hispaniola had begun her voyage to the Isle of Treasure. As for Long John, well, he still is the nicest cook...

SILVER: Do you want a sandwich?

JIM: That would be great, thanks Long John! *(SILVER exits; JIM addresses audience)* As you can see, Long John is a swell guy! Until...

(JIM hides in the corner)

Act 2 Scene 4

(enter SILVER and OTHER PIRATES)

JIM: *(to audience)* I overheard Long John talking to the rest of the pirates.

SILVER: Listen here you, Scallywags! I was with Captain Flint when he hid this treasure. And those cowards have the map. Follow my directions, and no killing, yet. Clear?

DICK: Clear.

SILVER: But, when we do kill them, I claim Trelawney. And remember, dead men don't bite.

GEORGE: Ay, ay, Long John!

(ALL exit but JIM)

JIM: *(to audience)* Oh no! Long John Silver IS the one-legged man that Billy Bones warned me about! I have to tell the others!

(JIM runs offstage)

King Lear for Kids

ACT 1 SCENE 1

KING LEAR's palace

(enter FOOL entertaining the audience with jokes, dancing, juggling, Hula Hooping... whatever the actor's skill may be; enter KENT)

KENT: Hey, Fool!

FOOL: What did you call me?!

KENT: I called you Fool.

FOOL: That's my name, don't wear it out! *(to audience)* Seriously, that's my name in the play!

(enter LEAR, CORNWALL, ALBANY, GONERIL, REGAN, and CORDELIA)

LEAR: The lords of France and Burgundy are outside. They both want to marry you, Cordelia.

ALL: Ooooooo!

LEAR: *(to audience)* Between you and me she IS my favorite child! *(to the girls)* Daughters, I need to talk to you about something. It's a really big deal.

GONERIL & REGAN: Did you buy us presents?

LEAR: This is even better than presents!

GONERIL & REGAN: Goody, goody!!!

CORDELIA: Father, your love is enough for me.

LEAR: Give me the map there, Kent. Girls, I'm tired. I've made a decision: Know that we - and by 'we' I mean 'me' - have divided in three our kingdom...

KENT: Whoa! Sir, dividing the kingdom may cause

chaos! People could die!

FOOL: Well, this IS a tragedy...

LEAR: You worry too much, Kent. I'm giving it to my daughters so their husbands can be rich and powerful... like me!

CORNWALL & ALBANY: Sweet!

GONERIL & REGAN: Wait... what?

CORDELIA: This is olden times. That means that everything we own belongs to our husbands.

GONERIL & REGAN: Olden times stink!

CORDELIA: Truth.

LEAR: So, my daughters, tell your daddy how much you love him. Goneril, our eldest-born, speak first.

GONERIL: Sir, I love you more than words can say! More than outer space, puppies and cotton candy! I love you more than any child has ever loved a father in the history of the entire world, dearest Pops!

CORDELIA: *(to audience)* Holy moly! Surely, he won't be fooled by that. *(to self)* Love, and be silent.

LEAR: Thanks, sweetie! I'm giving you this big chunk of the kingdom here. What says our second daughter, Our dearest Regan, wife to Cornwall? Speak.

REGAN: What she said, Daddy... times a thousand!

CORDELIA: *(to audience)* What?! I love my father more than either of them. But I can't express it in words. My love's more richer than my tongue.

LEAR: Wow, Regan! You get this big hunk of the kingdom. Cordelia, what can you tell me to get this giant piece of kingdom as your own? Speak.

 PlayingWithPlays.com

CORDELIA: Nothing, my lord.

LEAR: Nothing?!?

CORDELIA: Nothing.

LEAR: Come on, now. Nothing will come of nothing.

CORDELIA: I love you as a daughter loves her father.

LEAR: Try a little, harder, sweetie!

CORDELIA: Why are my sisters married if they give you all their love?

LEAR: How did you get so mean?

CORDELIA: Father, I will not insult you by telling you my love is like... as big as a whale.

LEAR: *(getting mad)* Fine. I'll split your share between your sisters.

REGAN, GONERIL, & CORNWALL: Yessss!

KENT: Whoa! Let's all just calm down a minute!

LEAR: Peace, Kent! You don't want to mess with me right now. I told you she was my favorite...

GONERIL & REGAN: What!?

LEAR: ...and she can't even tell me she loves me more than a whale? Nope. Now I'm mad.

KENT: Royal Lear, really...

LEAR: Kent, I'm pretty emotional right now! You better not try to talk me out of this...

KENT: Sir, you're acting ... insane.

Macbeth for Kids
ACT 2 SCENE 1

(DUNCAN runs on stage and dies with a dagger stuck in him, MACBETH takes his body off and then returns with the bloody dagger. LADY MACBETH enters)

LADY MACBETH: Did you do it?

MACBETH: *(clueless)* Do what?

LADY MACBETH: KILL HIM!

MACBETH: Oh yeah, all done. I have done the deed.

LADY MACBETH: *(pointing at the dagger)* What is that?

MACBETH: What?

LADY MACBETH: Why do you still have the bloody dagger with you?

MACBETH: Ummmmm, I don't know.

LADY MACBETH: Well go put it back!

MACBETH: NO! I'll go no more! I'm scared of the dark, and there is a dead body in there. I am afraid to think what I have done.

LADY MACBETH: Man you are a wimp, give me the dagger. *(LADY MACBETH takes the dagger, exits, and returns)*

LADY MACBETH: All done.

(there is a loud knock at the door)

LADY MACBETH: It's 2am! This really is not a good time for more visitors. *(goes to the door)* Who is it? *(opens door)*

MACDUFF: It is Macduff. I am here to see the king.

MACBETH: He is sleeping in there.

(MACDUFF exits while MACBETH and LADY MACBETH look at each other)

MACDUFF: *(offstage scream)* AGHHHHHHHHHHH – He's dead, he's dead!!! *(MACDUFF enters)*

MACBETH: Who?

MACDUFF: Who do you think? *(they both scream)*

BANQUO: *(BANQUO, MALCOLM, and DONALBAIN enter)* What happened, can't someone get a good night sleep around here?

MACDUFF: The king has been murdered.

MALCOLM & DONALBAIN: Aghhhhhhhh!!!!!!!!

DONALBAIN: We must be next.

MALCOLM: Let's get out of here.

DONALBAIN: I'm heading to Ireland.

MALCOLM: I'm off to England. *(MALCOLM and DONALBAIN exit)*

MACDUFF: Well, since there is no one left to be King, why don't you do it Mac?

LADY MACBETH & MACBETH: Okay. *(LADY MACBETH, MACBETH and MACDUFF exit)*

BANQUO: *(to audience)* I fear, thou play'dst most foully for't. *(MACBETH returns)*

MACBETH: Bank, what are you thinking over there?

BANQUO: Oh, nothing. *(said with a big fake smile)* Gotta go! See ya! *(BANQUO exits)*

ABOUT THE AUTHORS

KHARA C. BARNHART first fell in love with Shakespeare in 8th grade after reading Hamlet, and she has been an avid fan ever since. She studied Shakespeare's works in Stratford-upon-Avon, and graduated with a degree in English from UCLA. Khara is lucky to have a terrific career and a charmed life on the Central Coast of CA, but what she cherishes most is time spent with her husband and children. She is delighted to have this chance to help kids foster their own appreciation of Shakespeare in a way that is educational, entertaining, and most importantly, fun!

BRENDAN P. KELSO, came to writing modified Shakespeare scripts when he was taking time off from work to be at home with his newly born son. "It just grew from there". Within months, he was being asked to offer classes in various locations and acting organizations along the Central Coast of California. Originally employed as an engineer, Brendan never thought about writing. However, his unique personality, humor, and love for engaging the kids with The Bard has led him to leave the engineering world and pursue writing as a new adventure in life! He has always believed, "the best way to learn is to have fun!" Brendan makes his home on the Central Coast of California and loves to spend time with his wife and son.

CAST AUTOGRAPHS

Made in United States
Orlando, FL
16 November 2023

39039385R00057